Advance praise for
THE WINNING PORTFOLIO:
CHOOSING YOUR 10 BEST MUTUAL FUNDS
by Paul B. Farrell

"Dr. Farrell's book presents eminently practical advice for selecting mutual funds. His principles are carefully thought out and intelligent, and he correctly balances the case for actively managed funds versus index funds, all the while giving important emphasis to the critical variable of mutual fund costs. **THE ADVICE HE PROVIDES WILL HELP INTELLIGENT INVESTORS BUILD PRODUCTIVE MUTUAL FUND PORTFOLIOS.**"

> JOHN C. BOGLE
> Senior Chairman & Founder, The Vanguard Group
> Author of *Common Sense on Mutual Funds*

"Mutual funds are an important tool for investors planning for financial independence and **PAUL FARRELL'S NEW BOOK IS VERY WORTHWHILE READING.**"

> CHARLES R. SCHWAB
> Chairman & Co-CEO
> The Charles Schwab Corporation

"*The Winning Portfolio* presents an easy-to-follow roadmap for maximizing your mutual funds profits. **PAUL FARRELL'S UNIQUE APPROACH IS AT ONCE BOTH RATIONAL AND INTUITIVE.** This book presents a plan that any investor can stick to."

> BRIAN MURRAY
> Vice President & General Manager
> E*Trade Mutual Funds

"Paul Farrell is the Julia Child of mutual fund investing. **HIS CONCISE RECIPES FOR BUILDING A SOUND, SUSTAINABLE MUTUAL FUND PORTFOLIO ARE BOTH TASTY AND FINANCIALLY NUTRITIOUS.**"

TONY COOK
Managing Editor
Quicken.com

"Paul Farrell has written a quick-start manual that aptly introduces investors to both concepts and specific funds. **THIS BOOK IS A VERY GOOD READ.**"

A. MICHAEL LIPPER, CFA
President, Lipper Analytical Securities Corp.

"*The Winning Portfolio* articulates an investment plan that is easy to understand and simple to put in place. **THOSE WHO ACT UPON IT WILL BE WELL REWARDED.**"

FRED W. FRAILEY
Deputy Editor
Kiplinger's Personal Finance Magazine

"**PAUL FARRELL'S** *THE WINNING PORTFOLIO* **IS A MUST-READ FOR THE INDIVIDUAL INVESTOR LOOKING TO IDENTIFY, MONITOR, AND MAINTAIN A TOP-QUALITY MUTUAL FUND PORTFOLIO.** Similar to the research process at Janus, Mr. Farrell has 'dug deep' and gotten into the mindset of fund managers, backing his research with a blend of fact, figures, theory, and projections."

BLAINE ROLLINS
Manager, Janus Balanced and Janus Equity Funds

"It doesn't take a genius to see that *The Winning Portfolio: Choosing Your 10 Best Mutual Funds* by Paul Farrell is **A VERY VALUABLE TOOL FOR ALL MUTUAL FUND INVESTORS.**"

> L. ROY PAPP
> Chairman
> L. Roy Papp & Associates

"Paul Farrell's ten strategies for developing a long-term mutual fund investment program **ARE A MUST FOR THE NEW OR EXPERIENCED INDIVIDUAL INVESTOR.** Building a successful program for your fund portfolio using these strategies can be done by any investor willing to read this book."

> ALLAN R. TESSLER & ALAN J. HIRSCHFIELD
> Co-Chairmen & Co-CEOs
> Data Broadcasting Corp.

"Indundated by torrents of information about mutual fund supermarkets, 12b-1 fees, front and back end loads, with styles as diverse as mid-cap value and small-cap growth, no wonder investors are confused. **PAUL FARRELL'S *THE WINNING PORTFOLIO* DEMYSTIFIES THE MUTUAL FUND SELECTION PROCESS** by taking us behind the scenes of the SuperStar funds to meet the managers who earn the highest returns, and teaches us how to construct a portfolio whether we are baby boomers, retirees, or members of generation X."

> IVY SCHMERKEN
> Editor-in-Chief
> *Wall Street & Technology*

THE
Winning
PORTFOLIO

Also available from
BLOOMBERG PRESS

Investing in REITs:
Real Estate Investment Trusts
by Ralph L. Block

Staying Wealthy:
Strategies for Protecting Your Assets
by Brian H. Breuel

Investing with Your Values:
Making Money and Making a Difference
by Hal Brill, Jack A. Brill, and Cliff Feigenbaum

Investing in Small-Cap Stocks
by Christopher Graja and Elizabeth Ungar, Ph.D.

Don't Die Broke: How to Turn Your Retirement
Savings into Lasting Income
by Margaret A. Malaspina
(June 1999)

Investing in Hedge Funds:
Strategies for the New Marketplace
by Joseph G. Nicholas

The Inheritor's Handbook:
A Definitive Guide for Beneficiaries
by Dan Rottenberg

A Commonsense Guide to Your 401(k)
by Mary Rowland

The New Commonsense Guide to Mutual Funds
by Mary Rowland

Investing in IPOs: New Paths to Profit
with Initial Public Offerings
by Tom Taulli

BLOOMBERG PERSONAL BOOKSHELF

THE
Winning
PORTFOLIO

Choosing Your 10 Best
Mutual Funds

PAUL B. FARRELL

BLOOMBERG PRESS

PRINCETON

Books are available for bulk purchases at special discounts. Special editions or book excerpts can also be created to specifications. For information, please write: Special Markets Department, Bloomberg Press.

First edition published 1999
1 3 5 7 9 10 8 6 4 2

Farrell, Paul B.
    The winning portfolio: choosing your 10 best mutual funds / Paul
B. Farrell.
        p. cm. — (Bloomberg personal bookshelf)
    Includes index.
    ISBN 1-57660-071-8 (alk. paper)
    1. Mutual funds.   I. Title.   II. Series.
    HG4530.F365   1999
    332.63'27—dc21
                                                    98-52098
                                                        CIP

Acquired and edited by Jacqueline R. Murphy

To the new do-it-yourself investor:

"The most exciting breakthroughs of the twenty-first century will occur not because of technology but because of an expanding concept of what it means to be human."

—John Naisbitt, *Megatrends 2000*

"Think like an amateur.... If you invest like an institution, you're doomed to perform like one, which in most cases isn't very well.... If you're a surfer, a truck driver, a high school dropout, or an eccentric retiree, then you've got an edge already."

—Peter Lynch, *One Up on Wall Street*

"People ask me who is the best investor I know, and I say Will Brennan, 14. He's my son.... He has invested every month in a basket of equity funds, in good markets and bad, and he has made a fortune doing it. Why? Because he doesn't look at the market every day, and he doesn't react to news. He just invests regularly. The best investors are disciplined investors."

—John Brennan, CEO of Vanguard, in *Forbes*

"You need to do your own thinking. Don't get caught up in mass hysteria ... by the time a story is making the cover of the national periodicals, the trend is probably near the end.... Never listen to the opinions of others."

—Jack Schwager, *The New Market Wizards*

"I'm going to give you some advice about the stock market. Don't listen to any advice about the stock market."

—Andy Rooney, on *60 Minutes*

ACKNOWLEDGMENTS

TO ALLAN TESSLER and Alan Hirschfield, Data Broadcasting Corporation co-chairmen, and Jim Kaplan, president of Capital Management Sciences, a special thanks for giving me the opportunity of a lifetime.

To a couple of very special friends and partners, Craig Tolliver and Dennis Santiago: two who taught me so many new lessons about the relentless, daily process of creating and living in the on-line financial world.

To the CBS MarketWatch team for challenging me: Larry Kramer, CEO; Thom Calandra, editor-in-chief; Bill Bishop, new business chief; and Derek Reisfield, head of CBS New Media. Also my thanks to the desk editors—Alec Davis, Tom Murphy, and Tom Bemis—who work magic turning raw pages into readable prose.

To everyone at Lipper Inc.—especially Michael Lipper, Gary Kreissman, and Marcela Gaviria—for their friendship and their invaluable data.

To America's mutual fund writers, for setting the bar high: Fred Frailey, Manny Schiffres, and Steve Goldberg of *Kiplinger's;* Norman Fosback of *Mutual Funds;* Tom Petruno of the *Los Angeles Times;* Jonathan Clements of *The Wall Street Journal;* Jason Zweig of *Money;* Chet Currier of the Associated Press; John Waggoner of *USA Today;* Sheldon Jacobs of *No-Load Fund Investor;* Eric Kobren of *FundsNet Insight;* James Hagy of *Worth;* Howard Gold of *Barron's;* Eric Tyson; Russ Wiles; and so many others.

To Jim Bellows, my mentor at *The Los Angeles Herald-Examiner;* Michael Blodgett, a friend and mentor who has encouraged me as a writer for a long time; and Bill Griffeth of CNBC, my colleague from the Financial News Network.

To my longtime editor, Jacqueline Murphy, for continuing to make my greatest dreams come true, and the team at Bloomberg Press, including Melissa Hafner, Lisa Goetz, John Crutcher, Christina Palumbo, Maris Williams, and Barbara Diez.

To Dorothy, my wife and best friend; my son, Ian; and my siblings—Mary, Jeanette, Fred, and Michael—for their generous support and love. And most especially, Bill, Brian, and my many other friends in "the program" these past twenty-six years: you gave me my life and taught me to trudge the road to happy destiny. Thanks for the gift.

INTRODUCTION

Paradigm shifts. Cyberspace revolution. New millennium. The bull market. New world order. Information overload.

O WONDER investors are confused, overwhelmed, skeptical, and worried. Who wouldn't be, listening to all the noise competing for your attention throughout the press and the on-line media?

How can you pick the funds that are right for you? How can anyone build a winning portfolio? There are ten thousand mutual funds from which to pick. And hundreds of new ones crowding in every year. There are more four- and five-star funds today than there were total funds a decade ago. The fund world can seem like a three-ring circus.

Despite the insanity, you *can* build a winning portfolio. Anyone can, by using the basic principles in this book and the SuperStar 100 Funds—combined with common sense and a positive mental attitude.

This is *not* a book of clever tricks on how to get rich quick. Yes, you can become a millionaire—anyone can—but it takes a little discipline. This is also *not* a book about new cyber-technologies. As useful as computers are, you can build a very successful portfolio even without one. I do know there's an Internet revolution going on. It's all about nets and webs, computers and on-line technologies. I ought to know—I wrote three books about the Internet and cyberspace investing. Back in 1995, before most people even knew what "http://" meant, *Business Week* discovered and recommended my Web site as one of the best for investors.

For years I've written that the "cyberspace revolution" will transform life as we know it in the financial world, shifting power from Wall Street institutions to Main Street's individual investors. I also wrote at great length about all the incredible new on-line power tools, free databases, real-time news, unlimited quotes, on-line discount brokers, and other Web resources that are creating a new critical mass of individual investors.

That's all true. But the real paradigm shift is from technology to humanity. Today, computer technology and the Internet are not as important as you are. The new revolution is about *you*.

This book provides a simple, integrated approach to help you build a winning portfolio of mutual funds. There's nothing magical or complicated about the process. Your mental attitude is the key, not technology, not data. Stick to these principles and do it yourself.

Why did I write this book? Because I have faith in people. I believe that if people have the right tools and the best information, they'll take responsibility for their own financial futures. I believe that you can become a do-it-yourself investor and build a winning portfolio, all by yourself—without any professional help, and without dedicating your life to surfing the Web. And finally, I believe that when people take charge of their own financial destinies, they become stronger and more confident as individuals, family members, and citizens. Everybody wins.

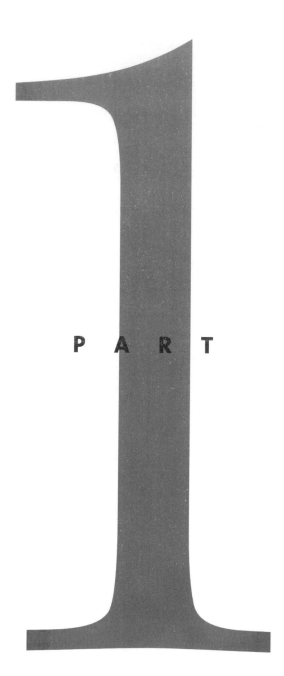

PART

Ten Rules in the New INVESTMENT FORMULA

T HE RULES IN THIS section are based on principles of living as well as investing.

DISCOVERING A KEEP-IT-SIMPLE WAY TO INVEST

THE TRUTH IS THAT most people earn the bulk of their money in some other way than by investing. In fact, when it comes to income, they would rather focus on what they know best—making money as, for example, a programmer, doctor, teacher, lawyer, or executive, not by playing the market all day.

What's the unstated goal here? It's simple: Most investors want to minimize the hours spent investing. They want to maximize portfolio returns with minimal risk. But most don't want to spend much of their precious time, if any, doing it, preferring that it happen almost automatically, like cruise control on a car.

Let's face it: After a full day of doing what we do best in business, we would rather be traveling on a weekend vacation in the Big Sur or Las Vegas, relaxing on a tropical beach, playing golf, enjoying dinner and a movie with friends, or hanging out with our children—or perhaps just zoning out in front of the television.

Very few people are *obsessed* about investing. But we do want the security and financial benefits that come from solid investment returns. We want a portfolio to support our life-style, not control our lives. Our investments, like the hundreds of little computers guiding our automobiles, should work in the background to make the journey safer and more fun—without our needing to think of them all the time as we head down life's highways.

I talk a lot about goals in this book—*my goal* is to help you achieve yours.

TEN RULES FOR SUCCESSFUL MUTUAL FUND INVESTING

PRINCIPLES ARE "LAWS OF the universe that pertain to human relationships and human organizations," says Stephen Covey in his classic best-seller, *Principle-Centered Leadership*. "They are part of the human condition, consciousness, and conscience. To the degree people recognize and live in harmony with such basic principles as fairness, equity, justice, integrity, honesty, and trust, they move toward survival and stability on the one hand or disintegration and destruction on the other."

Principles are at the core of what it means to be human, a way of life that empowers you. They are the compass guiding your life decisions in general, and your investment decisions in particular. They are an on-board guidance system that keeps you on the right path.

Here are the ten basic principles or rules that, when applied in a consistent, disciplined way, will help you build a winning portfolio and a secure future for you and your family.

Rule #1.   Be a Do-It-Yourself Investor.

Rule #2.   Start Auto-Pilot Savings Now.

Rule #3.   Max Out Your 401(k)—It's Your Best Investment.

Rule #4.   Focus on the Portfolio, Not the Funds.

Rule #5.   Buy and Hold—Forget Market Timing.

Rule #6.   Buy Cheap Funds—Low Cost, Low Risk, Low Stress.

Rule #7.   Inflation and the High Cost of Low-Risk Funds Can Kill You.

Rule #8.   Keep It (Very) Simple—Diversify Your Risks.

Rule #9. Past Performance Counts—It's the Best Tool You've Got.

Rule #10. Trust the Power Within Yourself, the Inner Winner.

Building a winning portfolio of mutual funds is not difficult, certainly not as difficult as most Wall Street professionals would have you believe. You need only six to ten funds to make this system work. In Part 2 I'll take a closer look at specific funds that you'll use to build a winning portfolio. But first, let's go through the steps that will help you build the framework to get you started.

Rule #1: Be a Do-It-Yourself Investor

BEING A DO-IT-YOURSELF investor means taking full responsibility for creating a portfolio of high-performance, low-cost mutual funds that you'll be able to hold on to for the long term.

MILLIONS OF AMERICAN investors are making the transition to self-directed investing. As Peter Lynch put it in *One Up on Wall Street,* "Rule #1, in my book, is: stop listening to professionals. Twenty years in this business convinces me that any normal person using the customary 3 percent of the brain can pick stocks just as well, if not better, than the average Wall Street expert. Think like an amateur. . . . If you're a surfer, a truck driver, a high school dropout, or an eccentric retiree, then you've got an edge already."

You can build a winning mutual fund portfolio by yourself, because all of the expertise you need is now available to you. Wall Street's historic monopoly over financial information no longer exists—investors today are not dependent on their brokers for tips or information resources. The power has shifted from Wall Street's institutions to Main Street America.

Discount brokerage first weakened Wall Street's stranglehold in the 1970s. On-line technologies widened the gap in the 1980s and 1990s. Now we're entering a new phase in this revolution, with the emergence of the self-reliant, self-directed investor.

The new do-it-yourself investors are taking control of their financial future. Armed with a new spirit of confidence, they are discovering the best tools to accomplish their goals and quickly learning how to use these tools to build successful portfolios. No-load, high-performing funds and other discounted services advance this new freedom.

A NEW AGE OF INSECURITY— RESULTING IN FINANCIAL SELF-RELIANCE

IN DECADES PAST, American investors relied on a variety of institutions—the government, our employers, and Wall Street—to guide us safely into retirement. They made the key financial decisions affecting our lives. Someone else had the information and the resources, so we were dependent on their authority and wisdom.

This is not the case today. Now we are moving through a new age of insecurity. Concerns about our financial futures are forcing American investors to become self-reliant. And we're rising to the challenge. Today, investors are not only financially savvy and computer-literate, we're also filled with a confidence that we can indeed manage our own financial future far better than any outside authorities, in government, corporate America, and Wall Street's institutions. It's easy with mutual funds.

AN EXPLOSION IN MUTUAL FUNDS

NOWHERE IS THIS TREND toward self-reliance and independence more obvious than in the explosive growth in the mutual funds owned by individual investors. Mutual fund assets have exploded almost tenfold since the mid-1980s, to over $5 trillion today, with $10 trillion projected for the early 2000s. By way of comparison, Fidelity Investments alone (the largest mutual fund family with almost $750 billion in assets under management) is now larger than the entire mutual fund market of the mid-1980s. And 75 percent of all fund assets are concentrated in the twenty-five largest fund families.

Today there are over 10,000 funds to choose from, a tenfold increase over the mid-1980s, with 500 to 1,000 new funds being added every year. In fact, there are now more four- and five-star top-performing funds than there were total funds a decade ago. As a result, advertisements for mutual funds are now so loaded with stars they look like ads for Hollywood movies.

FOUR PHASES IN AMERICA'S FINANCIAL REVOLUTION

Phase one. The advent of the discount broker in the mid-1970s marked the start of the individual investing revolution. Savvy investors suddenly had a bonanza of new options.

Phase two. Beginning in the early 1990s, the number of investors with on-line brokerage accounts at Schwab and the other on-line pioneers grew from fewer than 100,000 in 1993 to more than 5 million in five years. Fifteen million more are predicted for the early years of the next decade.

Phase three. The late 1990s have brought new on-line tools and the continuing proliferation of financial information—making it possible for individuals to manage the explosion in mutual fund choices. This has effectively diminished Wall Street's historic monopoly on financial information, and empowered individuals to take command of their portfolio choices.

Phase four. From 2000 on investment technologies will advance so rapidly that all investors will be on-line using power tools that automatically handle all the analysis, planning, portfolio monitoring, and trading, as do-it-yourself investing becomes the standard.

Investors' demand for new investment opportunities is so intense today that fund managers, brokerage firms, and financial advisers are doubling and tripling their advertising budgets to capture market share, and are routinely moving into the television and Internet media. Fueled by this increasing tide of new advertising monies, the major financial magazines are expanding coverage of mutual fund news substantially, providing their readers with more and better information with which to make financial choices. The cost is next to nothing compared with brokerage fees.

YES, YOU CAN DO IT YOURSELF

TRUE, THE AMOUNT OF information out there presents its own challenges. But the good news is that information continues to get better and cheaper. Investors are discovering a host of new keep-it-simple solutions, and not just through high-tech and on-line resources. Driven by a commercial need to sell their periodicals and to compete for ad dollars and readers, even the print media are transforming themselves into low-tech wholesale providers of professional-quality financial advice. Whatever you need to know about your mutual funds—it's out there and easy to get.

Being a do-it-yourself investor means using a total approach and focusing on mutual funds for the long term. It means integrating financial planning, simple asset allocation models, and disciplined portfolio management. Do-it-yourself investors should never chase the hot fund of the week or gamble their future on short-term market swings. They want funds and fund managers with long-term, proven track records.

Creating a winning mutual fund portfolio with the funds and asset allocation models provided in this book is an ideal way for investors to keep it simple and eliminate the cost of the middleman.

Burton Malkiel—member of the Council of Economic Advisers, former governor of the AMEX, and author of *A Random Walk Down Wall Street*—offers this bit of encouragement: "Many people say that individual investors have scarcely a chance today against Wall Street's pros. . . . Nothing could be further from the truth. You can do it as well as the experts—perhaps even better." Do it yourself.

Rule #2: Start Auto-Pilot Savings Now

AUTO-PILOT SAVING means developing the habit of automatically investing a percentage of your paycheck each month, *every* month.

THE KEY TO A SECURE financial future is disciplined savings. Start early and automatically put aside part of your income every month, no matter what. Save just $1,000 a year, starting at age twenty, and you'll have your million by age sixty-five. It's that simple. Along the way you'll achieve other goals, such as a family, a home, and college for your children. But many Americans wait too long to start. In fact, most are saving only about one-third of what they'll need to retire comfortably. The goal is to start early, and regularly save at least 10 percent of your income.

STUFF WE LEARN IN KINDERGARTEN THAT STICKS FOR A LIFETIME

BASIC TRUTHS, HUMAN VALUES, and fundamental principles are things we learned in kindergarten, or from our mothers or grandmothers. I learned the ultimate secret to successful investing as a kid, from the grandmother who raised me. Like many of her frequent reminders, though, it never quite sank in until years later. She said, "A penny saved is a penny earned." Simple advice, right? Actually, a penny saved is many pennies earned.

THE PERFECT GIFT FOR NEWBORNS

SAVE JUST $2.68 A WEEK and you'll retire a millionaire!

Why $2.68? I'm making a big point here, straight from Joel Wittenberg, a financial planning expert writing in *Your Money* magazine.

As preposterous as it sounds, that paltry sum is enough to make a new baby a millionaire by age 65. Try it; just put aside $2.68 a week in an index fund. Thanks to reinvesting plus compounding at about 10.5 percent (the long-term average return of the stock market), that $2.68 a week will grow into a $1 million in 65 years.

Think of what you can do for yourself at $100 a month; that's less than a Starbucks coffee and muffin a day, and less than the cost of a movie and dinner once a week. Just $25 a week, every week.

You'll sleep better—it's called peace of mind.

Charles Schwab put the message in perspective in one of his eight classic principles: *For every five years you put off investing, you may need to* double *your monthly investing amount to achieve the same retirement income.* Ouch.

SAVE AUTOMATICALLY: START NOW

MY GRANDMOTHER'S advice eventually penetrated. When I was a seventeen-year-old kid I joined the Marine Corps with one goal in mind: save enough money for college. My family didn't have the resources to assist me, but that didn't matter. I actually saved half of my salary for four years. It came right out of my paycheck; I never saw it.

You can do the same thing today. It's so simple, yet not all of us are putting this vital practice to work. Set up an automatic withdrawal from your bank account or paycheck. Save $100 and have it automatically sent to a

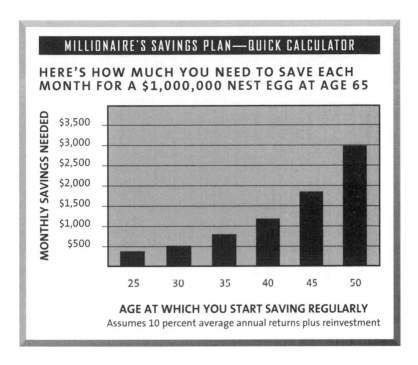

MILLIONAIRE'S SAVINGS PLAN—QUICK CALCULATOR

HERE'S HOW MUCH YOU NEED TO SAVE EACH MONTH FOR A $1,000,000 NEST EGG AT AGE 65

AGE AT WHICH YOU START SAVING REGULARLY

Assumes 10 percent average annual returns plus reinvestment

mutual fund, 401(k), or corporate dividend reinvestment program. It works: You'll have money for your future, and you'll be able to live well today, too. You only spend what you see, and the rest is automatically saved.

Between my savings, the G.I. Bill, part-time and summer jobs, scholarships, and loans, I put myself through ten years of higher education, including graduate school and law school, while raising a son. Later I even went back for a doctorate in psychology. I achieved my goals many times over, but it took a lot of discipline.

Yes, things are different today. A semester's tuition back then was about the cost of a Microsoft Windows upgrade today. But the principles are still the same.

Regular, disciplined saving is vital. The best way to save is to create an automatic deduction plan. That's the bottom line: Save more now. Enjoy life.

Rule #3: Max Out Your 401(k)—It's Your Best Investment

YOUR 401(K) IS THE best investment you'll ever make. You're virtually guaranteed to beat the markets easily.

PUT THE MAXIMUM amount allowable into your employer-sponsored 401(k) plan. It sounds too good to be true, but this opportunity virtually guarantees you a 50 percent minimum return on your money. What a gift. Your employer typically matches part or all of your contribution. It's also tax-deferred. You accumulate, compound, and reinvest your money without paying current taxes. Another gift. So between Uncle Sam (if your tax bracket exceeds 25 percent) and your boss (if he or she matches your contribution by 25 percent or more), you're making better than a 50 percent return on your money just by investing some of your income, even before you get any return on the investments themselves. Unfortunately, too many investors don't take advantage of this fabulous gift.

Why is your 401(k) such a perfect investment? Here are the four key advantages of these employer-sponsored programs:

1 Employer matching. Matching usually ranges somewhere between 25 percent and 150 percent of your contributions. There's nothing like free money being invested in your mutual funds.

2 Tax deferral. You'll enjoy this tax advantage for your contributions and also for the future earnings you reinvest in the plan.

3 Disciplined savings. 401(k)s are facilitated through automatic payroll deduction plans sent directly to your mutual funds or other investments.

4 Transferability. Once vested, the money is yours, even if you move to a new employer. You simply roll over your account into either an IRA or into your new employer's 401(k) plan, retaining your tax-deferral benefits.

These four benefits usually result in returns on your money that will exceed anything you earn by investing the same amount directly in the stock market.

In the table below you can see how much you'll have saved at age 65 if you start as a salaried employee making $25,000 at age twenty-five, receive 5 percent annual raises, and contribute 6 percent of your salary to a 401(k) plan that's earning you an average of 8 percent.

AGE AT START	AMOUNT AT AGE 65
25	$599,000
35	330,000
45	165,000
55	53,000

USEFUL RESOURCES

IF YOU HAVE DETAILED questions about your 401(k) options, I suggest that you buy Eric Schurenberg's book, *401(k): Take Charge of Your Future.* It's loaded with helpful hints, lists, forms, and schedules that'll get you on track with the best investment around. Right up front you'll see a chart that makes it absolutely clear why you should

THE FIVE BIGGEST 401(K) MISTAKES*

1 Failing to maximize your contributions. Hey, this is free money: you have to be crazy not to take it. If you put up nothing, the boss puts up nothing. If you put up the maximum, your boss puts up the maximum. And it's tax-deferred. Think of it this way: if you go to your local bank and they agree to give you a quarter for every dollar you deposit, would you do it? You bet. In a heartbeat.

2 Neglecting your asset allocations. Look closely at the specific allocations in your 401(k) portfolio. Most experts caution against investing heavily in your own company's stock. They also warn against the tendency to be too conservative and leave your money in fixed-income securities. Build a portfolio that reflects your investment goals. Also, review and rebalance your portfolio periodically to reflect shifts in the stock market that will throw your portfolio out of whack.

3 Playing the market as a stock trader. Conversely, paying too much attention to the market is also a minus. Recent bull market returns of 20 percent and more are making a lot of employees think that they can beat the market, so they become hot-shot traders. In an effort to maximize returns, investors often get obsessed about

start taking advantage of this gift immediately. Another great resource on 401(k)s is Mary Rowland's *A Commonsense Guide to Your 401(k)*.

Obviously, the earlier you start contributing, the better your life-style will be in retirement; and if you max out, you'll be a millionaire. Look at it another way: If you don't take advantage of the tax benefits and the matching contribution, you are foolishly throwing free money away.

Commit to investing the maximum allowable in your employer's 401(k) plan.

Start now, and max out your contributions. It's a simple way to get started in mutual funds.

timing the market, something even professional traders can't do consistently. Remember, you're creating a long-term, buy-and-hold retirement portfolio. This is not an opportunity to become a short-term trader or to "play the market."

4 Using your 401(k) as a bank lender. Most plans let you borrow against your accumulated assets at market rates. Resist the urge. You're saving for a future goal: retirement. Your 401(k) is not a bank; go somewhere else to borrow the money. Do not erase all your hard-earned savings by breaking into the piggy bank.

5 Making withdrawals that trigger unnecessary tax penalties. Remember, this is a plan designed for your retirement. If you take out money early, you'll pay not only ordinary income rates, but also a stiff 10 percent penalty. For example, if you change employers and you roll over your money into the new plan without paying off an outstanding loan beforehand, you may trigger a withdrawal and not realize it until it's too late.

* The steps here are based on Susan Kohn, "Avoid the Five Big 401(k) Mistakes," *Money* (September 1997).

Rule #4: Focus on the Portfolio, Not the Funds

ASSET ALLOCATION—the way you divide your money among investment alternatives—accounts for 90 percent of your portfolio's overall success.

DON'T LET STARS GET in your eyes. Fund management companies are stepping up their ad budgets. The pressure is on. Fund promoters will dazzle you with their hottest five-star funds, each with mouth-watering returns that will excite you. *"Pick our funds! Act now! Buy this hot fund of the week!"*

But wait. Research shows that 90 percent of your portfolio's returns are tied to your asset allocations. And less than 10 percent of your returns are tied to your fund-picking skills. In short, if you start with the right asset allocations—the ones that best fit your goals and needs—you could almost pick the right funds by throwing darts. Remember: You're building a winning portfolio, not just randomly picking the hot funds of the week.

DO YOU HAVE THE RIGHT ASSET ALLOCATIONS?

WHAT ARE YOUR ASSET allocations? Do you even know? Have you reviewed them lately? Do you know what *asset allocation* means?

If you're like most investors, your first instinct is to pick funds. But that's the wrong approach; you should take care of the fundamentals first. Picking funds, after all, is a slam-dunk—if you first take the time to structure your portfolio.

Here's how *Money* magazine put it in a February 1996 article by Eric Schurenberg:

> In a celebrated 1991 study, researchers Gary Brinson, Brian Singer, and Gilbert Beebower statistically proved what 90 percent of investing is. It is asset allocation—the way you divide your money among the investment options.
>
> The researchers found that the investment mix accounted for 91.5 percent of the variation in total return among the investors they surveyed. Security selection (whether the investor chose stocks or bonds that did better or worse than the pack) and market timing (when an investor decided to buy and sell) together explained a measly 6.4 percent of the difference in returns.

The bottom line: You need to plan your asset allocations very carefully. You can make a lot of mistakes deciding whether to pick this or that fund, and it won't matter as much as the mistakes you make if your asset allocations are wrong for you.

MODEL ASSET ALLOCATIONS

STRUCTURING A WORKABLE set of asset allocations isn't that difficult. We've all seen most of the key variations of these asset allocation models over the years. Most of the major mutual fund families and the major brokerage firms offer them.

For example, Fidelity and Vanguard began putting their interactive versions on America Online in 1994. They were the pioneers, along with the Charles Schwab brokerage and fund management firm. Since then, most of the other top-twenty-five fund families have played follow-the-leader on-line with a variety of services and planning tools, including model portfolios. Together these leading twenty-five fund families manage over 70 percent of the entire $5.5 trillion in mutual fund assets.

Unfortunately, fund families and brokers tend to be biased. Their own interests naturally come first. Like many investors, I am inherently skeptical of their materials.

The five model asset allocation profiles listed on the next page are a best-of-the-best consensus developed using all the research that went into the model portfolios I've seen on-line, drawing on ideas from the managers with America's top twenty-five fund families, and the best brokerage firms, plus the best ideas from the editors working with America's top financial periodicals.

CHOOSING THE RIGHT ASSET ALLOCATION MODEL

HERE'S WHAT THE EXPERTS SAY are the two most important factors in choosing your portfolio's asset allocations:

1 Timing/distance to target. How soon will you need the money?

2 Risk tolerance. How willing are you to risk losses?

You don't have to be a rocket scientist to grasp this principle of flexibility: if you have a lot of time and/or you are willing to accept higher downside risks in order to make higher upside returns, then you'll invest more in stocks than bonds and money-market instruments.

However, if you need the money soon and you want to protect your capital from losses, you'll forego a shot at the highest possible returns for downside safety. And your investments will definitely lean more toward fixed-income and money-market funds.

These profiles are the basis of the model portfolios presented in detail in Part 3. They are designed to help you move from the world of hypothetical models to build a real-world portfolio that fits your needs.

1 Income Preservation
2 Conservative Income
3 Growth and Income
4 Wealth Builder
5 Aggressive Growth

Let's look at the characteristics of all five of these portfolio types. I'll revisit these models in Part 3, when I explore ways to implement a portfolio that is a perfect fit for each of us.

WINNING PORTFOLIO #1: INCOME PRESERVATION

The "Income Preservation" portfolio is designed for investors with fairly immediate financial needs, usually less than two years, and/or those with a very low tolerance for market risk and volatility. This portfolio relies heavily on bonds, hybrid funds, and money-market funds. Stock funds that fit this model would most likely be solid blue-chip growth funds.

WINNING PORTFOLIO #2: CONSERVATIVE INCOME

The "Conservative Income" portfolio is also designed for investors who require a steady income flow. However, these investors also want some growth and capital appreciation. Since such investors have at least two to four years before they need the money, they're willing to take some modest risks, although probably few.

WINNING PORTFOLIO #3: GROWTH AND INCOME

This "Growth and Income" portfolio is structured for investors who want capital appreciation and don't need immediate income from their portfolio. Their tolerance for risk is moderate. With a medium-term time horizon of four to seven years—more than one average bull/ bear market cycle—these investors are willing to ride out near-term market fluctuations in search of reasonably solid growth and capital appreciation.

WINNING PORTFOLIO #4: WEALTH BUILDER

The "Wealth Builder" portfolio is designed for long-term investors seeking strong growth and appreciation in their portfolios. Because the time horizon of these investors is at least ten years, they are more interested in building future wealth than in current income. Returns are systematically reinvested.

WINNING PORTFOLIO #5: AGGRESSIVE GROWTH

The "Aggressive Growth" portfolio is designed for investors with a long-term horizon (more than a decade), plus patience and a strong tolerance for short-term risks and market fluctuations. Current income is not important.

I'll review these specific portfolio options and the funds that fit into them in detail in Part 3. But before I move on, let's review the process of connecting the model portfolios with actual funds listed in Part 2:

1 Select an asset allocation model that works for you.

2 Tack the Top-Ten SuperStar Fund lists from Part 2 on your wall.

3 Throw darts at these lists to pick your funds.

OK, so you refuse to throw darts to pick funds? I don't blame you. It will work if you have good lists, but there is a better way. I use the Dart-Throwing Strategy to illustrate the huge contrast between the facts that, in the long run:

◆ Over 90 percent of your portfolio's return is a direct result of your asset allocations, and

◆ Less than 10 percent depends on the specific funds you pick. So you *can* win by throwing darts at your asset allocations.

Moreover, note that the research underlying this asset allocation conclusion is based on picking funds from all the funds available—including the low performers—not just the SuperStar Funds presented in this book, not just a "best funds" list in *Kiplinger's* magazine, not just a limited selection of Morningstar's 5-star funds. All funds.

Your odds of success improve substantially once you narrow the list of funds you're considering from all 10,000 funds out there to an elite list of the very best.

That's when the Dart-Throwing Strategy starts making sense; mutual fund investing begins to become a no-brainer because more than 95 percent of your screening is done for you by experts who sift through the 10,000 funds and isolate the best 100. All the dogs are eliminated and you're simply picking from a list of known performers.

So, first determine your asset allocations, then begin to build a winning portfolio. Stay away from hot stocks and stick with the long-term performers that fit within your asset allocation needs.

Rule #5: Buy and Hold—Forget Market Timing

LONG-TERM INVESTING is the key to achieving your investment goals. Forget short-term market timing. You buy; you hold . . . and hold.

FORGET ABOUT TIMING the market; it doesn't work. You'll lose money. Invest for the long haul and then sit back and wait—the market always goes up in the long run. Don't let every market hiccup scare you into switching funds. Brokers, mutual fund advertisers, and others will constantly try to nudge you into short-term action. But the risks involved in guessing market swings far outweigh the potential profits. Most of Wall Street's top professionals agree: Market timing is a losing game for individual investors. Successful mutual fund investors buy and hold funds for the long term.

MARKET TIMERS ARE FROM MARS; BUY AND HOLD INVESTORS ARE FROM VENUS!

AT WHICH END OF THE spectrum are you most comfortable? There really are two quite different individuals involved in the market—the easy-going buy-and-hold variety and the gun-slinging, day-trading market-timers.

The vast majority of the 65 million mutual fund investors are of the buy-and-hold variety. They are basically conservative, infrequent traders with full-time careers and families that demand most of their attention. They car-pool, go to Little League games, enjoy tennis and golf; they teach school, drive trucks, carry mail, or otherwise work for a living. If you're reading this book you probably fall into this category of investors who should buy and hold for the long term.

By contrast, professional traders are a special breed. They love the thrill of the hunt. They love the game of playing the markets. In fact, it's more than a career to them, more than an addiction; it is their *destiny*. There are probably fewer than a million of these unique individuals in America, compared with the 70 million mutual fund shareholders.

How much can you improve your portfolio if you try your hand at market timing? Not much. Maybe you'll squeeze an extra 1 percent from the market if you're very lucky—but don't count on it. According to the Investment Strategies Network: "Attempts at timing often result in being 'in' or 'out' of the market at the wrong times. For example, data from Ibbotson Associates shows that if you had invested $1 in the stock market in 1926, that dollar would have been worth $1,114 at year-end 1995. However, if you had been out of the market for the best 35 months during that 1926–1995 period, your dollar would have returned just $10.16!"

EVEN TIMERS
MISS THE MARKET

WHY EVEN BOTHER trying to time the market? Even Joe Ricketts, CEO of AmeriTrade, agrees that market timing may not be worth it. He told *Fortune*: "The best thing, really, for an investor to do is buy a good company and hold it. . . . Trading often and heavy is not something that makes you a lot of money. That's contrary to my own interests, but it is the truth." And he should know. His company is one of the leading on-line discount trading firms.

Forget the market and its fickle short-term swings. Buy and hold . . . and hold.

Rule #6: Buy Cheap Funds—Low Cost, Low Risk, Low Stress

ALWAYS LOOK FOR FUNDS with no loads, low expenses, and low turnover. Avoid paying for services you can perform for yourself.

SHOP AROUND AND negotiate for the best prices on every mutual fund and every financial service you buy. Until fairly recently all financial advice and services were expensive, and Wall Street dictated the price. Yet Wall Street's monopoly on fees, advice, and information has now been virtually destroyed. Today, the average American investor can easily tap into the same resources as the professionals on Wall Street.

As the playing field levels, competition is creating exciting new low-cost opportunities in the financial services: no-load funds that reduce hefty brokerage commissions, no-fee fund supermarkets that allow you to build a portfolio from many families, low-cost index funds that beat most managed funds, low-low discount brokerage commissions, and much more. Discover the best bargains and you will substantially increase your returns.

THERE'S ALWAYS A CHEAPER, BETTER ALTERNATIVE

WHY PAY A 5 PERCENT load to a commissioned broker when you can always find a comparable or better-performing no-load fund? Why own a fund with 2 percent annual operating expenses when you can find others with expenses of only 0.20 percent? And why pick an actively managed fund run by a manager with a high turnover ratio that's jacking up your capital gains taxes and transaction costs? None of this makes any sense.

I interviewed Gus Sauter, manager of seven Vanguard funds. Here's his perspective on what you might save by investing in a low-cost, low-turnover index fund: "Making some reasonable assumptions: If you have a 20-year time

EIGHT RULES FROM THE MASTER OF THE CHEAP FUND

JOHN C. BOGLE, founder and chairman of the Vanguard mutual fund family, recommends putting your assets into low-cost, index mutual funds that simply follow the market benchmarks. In fact, Bogle's eight rules for picking funds are probably the most articulate statement of this investment philosophy. Commit them to memory:

Rule #1. Select low-cost funds. High expense ratios and 12b-1 (advertising) fees put a drain on higher returns. Favor low-turnover funds: Transaction costs and capital gains taxes on high turnover funds add to fund costs.

Rule #2. Beware of the added cost of advice. Buy no-load funds and avoid high commissions. Stay away from "wrap" accounts, often sold by brokerage firms and banks, adding annual management fees on top of existing fund commissions.

Rule #3. Do not overrate past fund performance. There is no way you can forecast future returns based solely on past performance.

Rule #4. Use past performance to determine risk. Look for consistency. Focus on funds with six to eight years in the top two quartiles and no more than one to two years in the bottom quartile of their peer group.

horizon, an actively managed fund would have to out-perform by about 2.5 percent to 3.0 percent per year in order to get the same after-tax returns. In other words, if the index fund returns 10 percent per year, the actively managed fund would have to return 12.5 percent to 13 percent to get the same after-tax returns for a buy and hold investor with a 20-year time horizon."

And to make matters even worse for most load-based funds, if you add in the impact of high turnover and a 3 percent to 5 percent up-front brokerage commission,

Rule #5. Beware of "stars." Few superstar managers are able to maintain the spectacular gains that earned them star status in the first place. Look for consistency and tenure.

Rule #6. Beware of asset size. When funds get too large, managers lose control. So-called economies of scale due to size are usually not realized, or not passed on to the investors.

Rule #7. Don't own too many funds. A portfolio that has too many funds results in overdiversification. This only increases cost and does little to minimize risk. How many funds are enough? Research shows that after twelve funds very little additional diversification is achieved.

Rule #8. Buy and hold. Investor emotions such as greed, fear, and hope can be just as destructive as negative market returns. Besides, market timing is a fool's game designed to humble the mighty.

OK, perhaps Bogle is biased toward Vanguard's approach. I would hope so. After all, he created it. Today his company has almost a half trillion dollars in assets under management, so apparently a lot of Americans agree with his philosophy.

the actively managed fund will have to return 15 percent just to break even with an index fund returning 10 percent, a 50 percent higher return. No wonder the vast majority of all actively managed funds never beat their indexes!

DON'T PAY FOR WHAT YOU CAN DO YOURSELF

FULL-SERVICE BROKERS claim that loads are what compensate them for their *advice*. Critics say the commission is mere payola to a hustling broker for selling you something that you probably don't need.

Don't need? That's right. Because if you can get an equivalent fund without paying an extra 5 percent broker's commission, and your adviser doesn't tell you, you're getting bad advice. The fact is, hundreds of no-loads consistently outperform load funds. It's no contest.

Check the math: When brokers make a sale, they get their percentage off the top, before you get a nickel's return. So with a load fund you're starting out with an immediate deficit. You pay in $100, but you have only $95 actually invested.

It's a good deal all right—but mostly for the broker.

The bottom line is that *you* keep the commission if you put your money in a no-load fund. It's that simple.

Rule #7: Inflation and the High Cost of Low-Risk Funds Can Kill You

IN THE PAST, retirees bought bonds for steady income plus safety. Today, they're forced into stock funds, just to stay even with inflation during the twenty-five or so years of retirement.

RETIREMENT IS TAKING on a whole new meaning in America. A retiree's portfolio must be built to last twenty-five years *and* be solid enough to beat inflation. Major trends are changing the rules of the game. People are living longer, healthier lives. With financial planners reminding us we need a million bucks to retire in style, a savings shortfall is forcing many to plan carefully and, sometimes, take greater risks. This new paradigm is making us acutely aware of the harsh reality that our investments demand a more aggressive strategy.

BALANCING RISKS: SHORT TERM VERSUS LONG TERM

WHEN IT COMES TO retirement planning, inflation can be a portfolio killer if you have too much money in low-return bonds or cash. Of course, the point of investing your savings is to beat inflation by taking some calculated risks on the market. But market cycles, too, can present short-term challenges in the event of market volatility.

INFLATION AND YOUR INVESTMENT RETURNS

HISTORICALLY:

◆ Inflation averages 4.5 percent.

◆ Bonds (both Treasury bills and long corporate bonds) average between 6.5 and 7.5 percent.

◆ Stocks return about 10.6 percent.

Here's where the trade-off comes in: Some retirees expect to live off of a portfolio that is invested heavily in aggressive funds. But if the market drops 15 to 20 percent, and stays there for several months—or worse, a year or more—the planned income from aggressive investments can disappear. Alternatively, if you have very low-risk investments, you'll need to calculate the likelihood of their keeping pace with inflation. It's always a balancing act between inflation and market risks. But you do have various options, depending upon your choice of strategy and risk tolerance.

BECOMING A
RESPONSIBLE INVESTOR

BE PRUDENT. Don't throw caution to the wind by putting your entire retirement portfolio in high-risk stocks. On the other hand, avoid being too cautious. Plan for cash reserves, but don't stuff all of your money in a low- or no-yield mattress.

Rule #8: Keep It (Very) Simple— Diversify Your Risks

DIVERSIFICATION IS ONE of the key reasons investors choose mutual funds to build their portfolios. Diversification minimizes risks and maximizes returns as you spread your money across 50 to 500 stocks. In addition, professional managers make the hard decisions to buy and sell individual stocks.

HOW MANY FUNDS ARE enough? Or too many? What's the minimum? Here's a sampling of the wide range of decisions made under different conditions:

◆ The Investment Company Institute (the primary trade association for major mutual fund families) reports that 57 percent of all investors actually own three funds or fewer, 26 percent own four to six funds, and only 15 percent have seven or more funds.

◆ *Fortune* reports that quite the opposite is true with well-heeled investors. Citing a study from Kobren Insight Group, among investors who had more than $500,000 in fund investments, some 78 percent had at least ten funds and a 45 percent had more than fifteen. In short, high-net-worth investors may be unnecessarily overdiversified.

◆ Our CBS MarketWatch team did a similar survey of our readership. The majority (54 percent) of the investors in our study had between six and eleven funds in their

HOW TO CREATE A DE FACTO INDEX FUND

A WORD OF CAUTION: one investor sent us his portfolio of 46 funds. Keep in mind that if the average fund has 125 to 150 stocks, and there was no duplication, this portfolio could have as many as ten times the number of stocks as the S&P 500! Another portfolio we analyzed had 26 funds.

These extreme attempts at mega-diversification are counterproductive, costly, and self-defeating. In effect, these portfolios themselves were pseudo-index funds. We advised these two investors to rebalance and get into a diverse group of ten index funds covering blue-chip, small-cap, international, and fixed-income holdings, using the asset allocations in their financial plans. That would more efficiently accomplish the same results, with fewer administrative and accounting headaches. All this assumes, of course, that the tax consequences of this rebalancing are favorable.

portfolios. Academic research confirms this is an acceptable range to achieve diversification.

Remember: Fewer than five funds and you probably won't get enough diversification for a solid portfolio. But if you invest in more than twelve funds, you won't be adding any new diversification, although you *will* be increasing costs, management problems, and your level of anxiety.

SOMETIMES TEN FUNDS ARE NO BETTER THAN ONE

YOU CAN ALSO HAVE TEN funds and still get no more diversification than you might in a single fund—if they're all mimicking one another. Here's a simple example. Suppose you invest in ten S&P 500 index funds. Obviously they're all going to be weighted with exactly the same 500 blue-chip stocks, so you are simply duplicating the same fund ten times over, while increasing your reporting and management headaches.

That's not to say that you can't have your entire portfolio in index funds. Many investors do. It's a strategy that makes sense, many experts argue, because the majority of all fund managers do not beat their indexes. Therefore, why go with a managed fund? Stick with the indexes.

The point is, you should diversify your portfolio so as not to pick funds that all provide the same level of risk and performance at the same time.

SOME EXCEPTIONAL CONTRARIANS ARE BREAKING THE RULES

ALTHOUGH THE GURUS OF diversification emphatically tell us that any portfolio with more than twelve funds is getting no more diversity of risk exposure, a few noted experts are ignoring the rules.

Arthur Levitt. A couple of years ago, SEC Chairman Levitt had a portfolio of $15 million in seventeen funds. That's almost $1 million per fund. Levitt is the "top cop patrolling America's mutual funds," in the words of *Mutual Funds* magazine. He was a successful, wealthy investor before entering public life, as president of Shearson Hayden Stone, and he also served as chairman of the American Stock Exchange for sixteen years.

He was solidly diversified with over nine domestic stock funds, including four international and four fixed-income funds. Perhaps equally noteworthy is the fact that all of his funds were no-load funds and funds with below-average expense ratios.

It is also interesting to note that seven of his funds were not four- or five-star funds, using the Morningstar ratings. Levitt accomplished diversification by spreading his risk across many markets, styles, and capitalization sizes.

Sheldon Jacobs. Similarly, Sheldon Jacobs, publisher of the *No-Load Fund Investor* newsletter and one of the most highly respected mutual fund experts, has fourteen funds in his personal portfolio. In addition, he has eleven bonds (four municipal bonds and seven zero-coupon U.S. Treasury bonds), a strategy that probably makes sense for someone in a high-income-tax bracket. Jacobs has no bond funds and no stocks.

Both Levitt and Jacobs are pros with portfolios outside the norms, thus supporting the idea that diversification itself is more important than the number of funds or the statistics in some academic research studies. Of course, at seventeen or fourteen funds, neither investor had gone too far outside the recommended upper limit of twelve funds.

The lesson here is simple: You, the individual investor, must feel comfortable in your gut with the number of funds you choose for your portfolio, regardless of what the rules say.

Robert Torray. At the other end of the spectrum is Robert Torray, one of the more successful mutual fund managers in the industry. His $1.4 billion fund returned 38 percent in a recent three-year period. In an interview I asked Torray the following question: If an investor were to build a portfolio with the Torray fund as its core, what percentage of the portfolio should it represent? He stated rather boldly that it ought to be 100 percent. "I don't believe in asset allocation to begin with," he went on to say.

Torray noted that even if you pick four or five funds, the average fund has 125 to 150 stocks in it, so you end up with 500 to 750 stocks. You may as well be in an index fund. The Torray Fund is a focused no-load value fund with only forty investments, a low 20 percent annual turnover, and average annual returns of 25 to 30 percent, so it's hard to fault his approach.

As if to punctuate the point, Torray exclaimed, "I personally own only nine stocks plus the fund, and all nine stocks I own are in the fund! I got everything I have in them and I sleep soundly. We don't have one loser."

THE BOTTOM LINE:
PICK TEN FUNDS THAT
WORK WELL TOGETHER

MY RECOMMENDED range for most investors is to shoot for six to ten funds. If you really want to do it right, why not choose a perfect grouping of ten funds? That will give you a solid, well-diversified mutual fund portfolio. Assuming you start with the right asset allocations for your investor profile, and work with a database of long-term top performers like the ones listed in this book, you will be able to build a winning long-term portfolio.

Rule #9: Past Performance Counts— It's the Best Tool You've Got

THE PAST PERFORMANCES of the fund and of its manager are the two best indicators of the probable success you can expect from your investment.

EVERYONE HAS HEARD the warning, *Past performance does not guarantee future results.* This mantra is automatically inserted in every prospectus and often repeated in public. Yet, historically, it's the one rule everyone honors in the breach. Why? While not perfect, past performance is actually one of our *best* predictors of future results. In fact, individual and institutional investors, professionals and academicians, all rely heavily on past performance in their investment decisions. The manager's career stock-picking performance is the other major predictor of future results. The manager's tenure, consistency of style, and long-term performance are critical indicators in predicting the fund's future performance.

BET ON THE JOCKEY

TOP-RANKED JOCKEYS typically ride atop the best horses. Willie Shoemaker rode more than 40,250 races, winning 8,833, including 4 Kentucky Derbys. Do you want to win the portfolio race? Then keep it simple: Find managers with winning track records who are managing funds that record solid performance over several continuous years—and place your bets!

A few years ago *Mutual Fund* magazine surveyed 100 professional money managers. Pros picking pros. What were their most reliable criteria in selecting a winner? Here's their idea of the top three most reliable criteria for picking a mutual fund, in rank order:

1 Long-term track record. A consistent ten-year track record of returns.

2 Consistent management style. Managers with a clear and focused investment strategy.

3 Tenure of portfolio managers. A manager who has longevity, including bear market experience—something less than 15 percent of today's money managers have.

Commit these three criteria to memory: They are vital to your success.

THE RULE EVERYONE BREAKS

IN THE FINAL ANALYSIS, past performance matters a lot to the average investor walking down Main Street—regardless of the conventional wisdom (and the SEC). You have to remain vigilant, however. Check all research stats yourself. The fact is, fund managers sometimes let successful bouts of past performance go to their heads. They spend more time on promoting and less on educated stock picking.

It's true that almost half of the funds which generate impressive returns don't finish in the top half two years in a row. But the other half do repeat as top performers —and some outperform year after year after year.

This characterizes one criterion I used to assemble the SuperStar Funds listed in Part 2. These funds are perennial winners, prescreened from the complete list of 10,000 funds. I chose the best of the best. These are the top funds available, being managed by some of the best professionals on the Street.

Rule #10: Trust the Power Within Yourself, the Inner Winner

INVESTING IS NOT as complicated or as mysterious as Wall Street wants you to believe. Trust your inner power and you will make the right choices for your future.

"WHETHER YOU WIN OR lose, you are responsible for your own results. Even if you lost on your broker's tip, an advisory service recommendation, or a bad signal from the system you bought, you are responsible. . . . Do your own thinking. . . . Never listen to the opinions of others."

As Jack Schwager reminds us in his classic, *The New Market Wizards,* whether you come out ahead or you lose your shirt, you are responsible for your own results. Fortunately, a new science of investment psychology is emerging to help investors deal with the mental stresses and anxieties traveling in the wake of the worldwide financial revolution. Indeed, the principles of this new investment psychology directly reflect the new spirit of the independent do-it-yourself investor.

The key to financial success is rapidly shifting from the left brain to the right brain—from technology and quantitative solutions, to educated intuition, mental discipline, and keep-it-simple common sense.

In searching for ways to deal with today's information overload, along with the responsibilities of planning and managing for the future, I have discovered the roots of this new discipline in an odd assortment of books (listed below), each of which covers a separate but equal piece of the investment-psychology puzzle.

All of these may not be your cup of tea, but take a look at them as you browse through your local bookstore. The majority are not even focused exclusively on managing your investments. What they all *do* address, however, is the much trickier feat of managing your expectations, conquering your fears, and learning to trust your instincts. If you want to master your money, learn to master your own emotions.

Listening to your inner voice is a huge part of success in investing and, indeed, in life. As Wayne Dyer put it in *Real Magic,* "Most of us believe that moneymaking is a game that is played with forces outside ourselves, forces

BOOKS ON INVESTMENT PSYCHOLOGY

- ◆ *Awaken the Giant Within: How to Take Immediate Control of Your Mental, Emotional, Physical, and Financial Destiny*, by Anthony Robbins
- ◆ *The Disciplined Trader: Developing Winning Attitudes*, by Mark Douglas
- ◆ *The Inner Game of Trading: Creating the Winner's State of Mind*, by Robert Koppel and Howard Abell
- ◆ *Investment Psychology Explained: Classic Strategies to Beat the Markets*, by Martin Pring
- ◆ *The Road Less Traveled: A New Psychology of Love, Traditional Values, and Spiritual Growth*, by M. Scott Peck
- ◆ *Zen Guitar*, by Philip Toshio Sudo

For more information on these and other books of value, see the reading list at the end of this book. In the final analysis, however, the secret power is within you, not a book. Discover it, trust it, listen to it, live by it.

such as the economy, the stock market, interest rates, the Fed, government policies, employment statistics, and the like. But as you move along a spiritual path and begin to get a taste of the power of your invisible self, you discover that moneymaking is merely a game that you play with yourself. . . . Money is not a goal unto itself. If you chase after it, it will always elude you."

PART

2

America's
Top-100
SUPERSTAR
FUNDS

THERE ARE TOO many funds, too many choices, and too few winners. Over ten thousand mutual funds are available to you—ten times the number you had to choose from back in the 1980s.

WHY SUPERSTAR FUNDS? INFORMATION OVERLOAD

IT'S NO WONDER THE biggest complaint I hear today from investors is about "information overload." The mutual fund stratosphere is littered with junk, which is guaranteed to create even more frustration in the near future, as five hundred to a thousand new funds are being added every year. Unfortunately, not only are there too many funds; as it turns out, most of them are also substandard performers. More than 80 percent of all mutual funds fail to beat their relevant market indexes.

Fortunately, an elite group *does* shine brightly above the vast wasteland. That's why "best funds" lists—like the one we've researched and compiled here—have become so useful to individual investors. They help you narrow down your choices to the best of the best. Still, investors do need help navigating the stormy sea of multiple "best funds" lists.

SELECTING THE TOP-100 SUPERSTAR FUNDS: FOUR CRITERIA

HERE'S HOW THE SuperStar Funds directory works. It's actually quite simple:

1 Respected national and financial periodicals. Our CBS MarketWatch Mutual Fund Center now monitors more than thirty major financial magazines, newspapers, and advisory newsletters on a daily basis. Lists of these publications are prepared by the top

editors and experts in the mutual funds business—
sources we believe are truly objective.

The financial periodicals we monitor are published
daily, weekly, or monthly. However, although most of the
"best funds" lists that we monitor are published on a regular basis as feature items for investors, perhaps a third
of them are occasional recommendations.

2 Top-performing funds and top-gun managers. Our
approach to building a mutual fund portfolio is based on
long-term financial planning and asset allocations. We
discourage chasing the "hot fund" of the week. Hence, we
eliminate all funds that lack established track records. All
of the funds we select have long-term performance records
of at least 3 years, and usually 5 to 10 years or longer. The
SuperStars on this track are proven jockeys riding proven
horses.

3 Multiple selection criteria. The "best funds" lists we're
tracking use a variety of objective screening processes,
analytical approaches, and decision-making criteria. In
this way, the SuperStar consensus directory helps investors
identify which "best funds" are the "best of the best" from
the objective viewpoints of America's top-gun investment
experts.

4 Diversification across multiple databases. The selection
of the specific databases used in assembling each of the
"best funds" lists that underlie our SuperStar directories is
made independently by the individual editors compiling
each particular list. Thus no one database is preferred by
our system.

In the process, we believe our SuperStar Funds consensus directory tends to screen out statistical biases and
data variations that might be inherent in the six most
popular mutual fund databases—Lipper, Morningstar,
Micropal, Value Line, CDA/Wiesenberger, and the
Institute for Econometric Research. At the same time,
this process draws on the experiences of over one hun-

dred and fifty separate groups of experts in any one year. Fortunately, all of the major rating agencies and their databases are represented in the "best funds" lists we monitor.

Our list of SuperStar Funds consists of the best funds in these seven major categories:

◆ **Thirty top stock funds.** This category includes the top growth, equity-income, growth and income, and value-oriented growth funds.

◆ **Ten top higher-risk equity stock funds.** This group includes aggressive-growth, small-cap, and capital-appreciation funds.

◆ **Ten top global and international funds**

◆ **Ten top sector stock funds**

◆ **Ten top hybrid funds.** This list includes balanced, asset allocation, and convertible funds.

◆ **Ten top index funds**

◆ **Twenty top fixed-income bond funds.** This group includes corporate bond, U.S. government treasuries, and tax-exempt municipal bond funds.

Blue-Chip Stock Funds

OVER 65 PERCENT OF all large-cap stock funds are in three peer groups: growth, equity-income, and growth and income. About $2.0 trillion is invested in these few basic, conservative categories of funds. Risk is moderate while the returns are moderate to high over the long term.

YOUR PORTFOLIO'S CORE FUNDS

THE DIFFERENCES between these three equity categories are more often a matter of degree than of fundamentals. All invest for long-term growth through capital appreciation, dividend growth, or some combination of the two. Typically, each of them invests in established companies with name brands familiar to the average investor. These funds are often the first choice in many portfolios, especially for new investors.

In actual practice, the distinctions among these three categories are often very blurry, although as an asset class they are quite different from higher-risk funds, such as aggressive growth, small-cap, sector, and global funds.

◆ **Growth funds** seek capital growth. Dividend income is not a significant factor. They invest in common stocks that are well established and demonstrate solid earnings growth. Growth stocks typically trade at high multiples of earnings.

◆ **Value-oriented growth funds** look for stocks with low price-to-earnings ratios and low valuations to earnings, with high yields. Their growth is based on long-term capital appreciation rather than current earnings growth.

◆ **Growth and income** funds seek to combine long-term capital growth and current income. They invest in the common stocks of companies that have a solid record of paying dividends and increasing share values.

◆ **Equity-income funds** are seeking a high level of income by investing mainly in companies with strong histories of dividend payments.

Investors tend to put most of their money into these categories of funds. They are conservative, middle of the road funds in terms of risk and returns—first and foremost, they yield peace of mind. There are no nerve-wracking microcaps, no volatile aggressive-growth swingers, and no "hot funds of the week." In fact, many of these Growth Fund SuperStars are as safe and as boring as bonds. The statistics reported here will obviously vary over time, but they should nevertheless give you a fairly accurate impression of the Top-100 Super-Stars.

SUPERSTAR STOCK FUNDS: GROWTH AND VALUE

AARP/SCUDDER GROWTH & INCOME

When the American Association of Retired Persons (AARP)—a conservative, nonprofit organization with over thirty million members—wanted to develop mutual funds for its members, baby boomers 50 years old and over, they went to Scudder. Scudder pioneered the no-load approach, offering America's first no-load mutual fund to investors in 1928.

The lead manager of the AARP Growth & Income Fund, Rob Hoffman, also manages AARP's Balanced Fund and the Scudder Growth & Income Fund, which is virtually identical except that it invests in some less socially conscious companies. AARP Growth & Income buys value and sells growth. As Hoffman put it, "We buy

SUPERSTAR GROWTH AND VALUE FUNDS

LARGE-CAP, MIDCAP, AND BLUE-CHIP

1 AARP/Scudder Growth & Income
2 American Century–Twentieth Century Ultra
3 American Century Income & Growth
4 Babson Value
5 Dodge & Cox Stock
6 Domini Social Equity
7 Excelsior Value & Restructuring
8 Fidelity Dividend Growth
9 Fidelity Equity-Income
10 First Eagle Fund of America
11 Gabelli Growth
12 Gabelli Westwood Equity Retail
13 Harbor Capital Appreciation
14 Janus Twenty
15 Legg Mason Value Primary
16 Mairs & Power Growth
17 Neuberger & Berman Partners
18 Nicholas Fund
19 Oakmark Fund
20 Papp America-Abroad
21 Safeco Equity No-Load
22 Selected American Shares
23 Sound Shore Fund
24 T. Rowe Price Dividend Growth
25 T. Rowe Price Equity-Income
26 T. Rowe Price Mid-Cap Growth
27 Torray Fund
28 Vanguard Growth & Income
29 Vanguard Windsor II
30 White Oak Growth Stock

value, and we're smart enough to hold it while it's growing. Then we force ourselves to sell it when that growth causes the stock price to outstrip any dividend increases that may have occurred and it's starting to stretch valuation."

With about $7 billion invested, they've averaged around 20 percent returns in recent years. A $10,000 investment in this fund a decade ago would be worth about $50,000 today. Turnover is low: under 30 percent. Expenses are just 0.75 percent, compared with a peer-group average closer to 1.25 percent. And beta is a modest 0.82. (Beta measures volatility against the S&P 500, which has a beta of 1.00.) This fund is a solid performer.

For more information call 1-800-322-2282

AMERICAN CENTURY–TWENTIETH CENTURY ULTRA

American Century's no-load Ultra has been around since 1981, and it has grown to almost $25 billion in recent years. To accommodate the growth, Ultra has transformed itself from a small-cap (stocks with market capitalizations under $1 billion) into a large-cap (over $5 billion) fund. Meanwhile, performance has remained surprisingly consistent. Ultra's average returns were a solid 20 percent plus for the last 10 years, and an initial $10,000 investment would now be worth about $80,000 today. Annual expenses are a modest 1.00 percent. Turnover is slightly over 1.05 percent. Beta is about 1.20, indicating higher than normal volatility, which is common with growth funds.

In spite of its exceptional growth, American Century Ultra has remained true to its "growth" investment philosophy. It focuses on large-caps with steady earnings growth, offering an excellent counterpoint to the value-oriented equity funds. Value managers buy companies at a discount, almost on speculation, and hold on to them for a long period, hoping that the stocks' performance will improve. When the value of such stocks then increases to the point at which they would be considered growth stocks, they are sold off. As John Sykora, one of Ultra's team managers, put it, "Our growth-oriented style has a higher turnover than the value funds. We're moving to where the earnings are and where earnings are accelerating." Ultra was a great small-cap, and guess what? It's a pretty good large-cap.

For more information call 1-800-354-2021

AMERICAN CENTURY INCOME & GROWTH

Although this fund has been around since 1990, the relentless bull market coupled with a solid performance record has been drawing in new investors, pushing its assets well past $3 billion. Back in mid-1997 Income & Growth turned the reins over to comanagers John Schniedwind and Kurt Borgwardt, both veterans with American Century's family of sixty funds. The fund's stated goal is to beat the S&P 500 index by a couple of points. And they have indeed. A $10,000 investment at inception in 1990 would have been worth about $45,000 after 7 years. Average annual returns have been almost 30 percent for the recent 3-year period, and above 25 percent for 5 years.

This team hit the ground with both feet running and hasn't missed a step. Schniedwind and Borgwardt have a value-oriented portfolio. The core of their investment style, however, is a cold and calculating quantitative model that scans their database of 1,500 large stocks using a bottom-up approach—that is, looking for low valuations plus promising earnings momentum. Once in the portfolio (with another 300 or so stocks), these holdings are watched in a disciplined manner as the managers maintain their database of new opportunities.

As a result, with turnover roughly 100 percent a year (higher than that of most buy-and-hold funds), and with about three hundred stocks in the portfolio, volatility and beta match those of the benchmark S&P 500, and expenses hover around 0.75 percent. The prospect of achieving high returns at a modest risk will surely continue to draw in new investors hooked on the thrill of beating the index.

For more information call 1-800-345-2021

BABSON VALUE

Manager Nick Whitridge has been at the helm of the Babson Value fund since its inception in 1984. He runs a tight ship, focusing on about forty large-cap blue chips in a portfolio of about $1.5 billion in assets. Whitridge is a solid value-oriented buy-and-hold investor, confident on both the buy and the sell side, and his fund has posted low turnover (in the 20 percent range) in recent years. His long-term performance is consistently strong, averaging around 20 percent for a recent 3-year period, and about 15 percent for the past decade. A $10,000 investment 10 years ago would be worth well over $50,000 today.

How does he do it? Whitridge's radar is constantly scanning his universe of 1,600 companies, searching for opportunities. His screening criteria help him selectively target a narrow list of fewer than a hundred stocks for more detailed fundamental analysis. His goal: uncover assets that have strong upside potential and that the market is ignoring or heavily discounting. From there, Whitridge's experience takes over. He's totally confident in his ability to pick the right companies—stocks that are prime candidates to take off and zoom across the market's radar. Having made the buy decision, Whitridge disciplines the portfolio, staying within tight weightings of 2.5 percent for each of the portfolio's forty stocks. Whitridge's precision has paid off handsomely for investors looking for solid large-cap opportunities.

For more information call 1-800-422-2766

DODGE & COX STOCK

Ready to play tennis or travel the world without any port-folio worries? Do you want to just park your money and forget it, knowing it's in secure hands for the long haul? Then give John Gunn a call; he's been with the firm since earning his MBA from Stanford in 1972. He's lead manager of the Dodge & Cox Stock Fund, which has been around since 1965, managing about $4 billion in assets. This team has been so consistently good for so long, they're boring! Listen to these stats. Expenses are under 0.60 percent. The fund is highly tax-efficient: For the past decade or more, turnover has been hovering around 20 percent or less. And volatility is under that of the benchmark S&P 500. Total returns have been over 15 percent for a 15-year period, and about 20 percent for a recent 3 years. A $10,000 investment a decade ago would be worth over $50,000 today.

How do they do it? It's simple: Dodge & Cox, the ulti-mate buy-and-hold investor, picks solid value and hangs on for dear life, as my grandmother used to say. They buy great brand-name, market-leading blue chips when they are undervalued, like GM, Citigroup, Dow Chemi-cal, Kmart, Alcoa, and American Express. Then they wait for the recovery cycle.

OK, so bargain stocks are becoming scarcer in today's pricey market. But somehow these guys do find them while screening for opportunities in out-of-favor sectors, then using their highly disciplined bottom-up funda-mental analysis. Dodge & Cox Stock is a great choice for ultraconservative investors who want a fund they won't lose any sleep on, while they go about enjoying life.

For more information call 1-800-621-3979

DOMINI SOCIAL EQUITY

If you have a strong social conscience, I encourage you to read *Investing for Good: Making Money While Being*

Socially Responsible. The book was published in 1993 by authors Peter Kinder, Steven Lydenberg, and Amy Domini, shortly after they created the Domini Social Equity Trust. At first the trio was dismissed as merely New Age liberals by many individual investors, institutions, corporations, and journalists, although Kinder is a lawyer and Lydenberg a securities analyst.

Guess what? They proved their point. You *can* make money and do good at the same time! Performance of the Domini Social Equity Fund in recent years has matched or surpassed benchmarks: annualized returns of around 25 percent and 20 percent for the past 3 and 5 years, respectively. Meanwhile, turnover is a low, low 5 percent. If you'd invested $10,000 in Domini Equity at inception in 1991, you'd have had around $35,000 within 7 years. That beats the average growth and income fund at about $25,000, and it's virtually neck and neck with the S&P 500 over the same period—a benchmark that most actively managed equity funds can't beat. That kind of performance is "doing good" for your retirement portfolio, as well as "doing good" for society!

For more information, see a brand new book that is packed with the best information on socially responsible funds: *Investing with Your Values: Making Money and Making a Difference,* by Hal Brill, Jack A. Brill, and Cliff Feigenbaum, with a foreword by Amy Domini.

There are now over sixty socially responsible funds. Funds like the Domini Fund give investors the right vehicle to invest with integrity—according to their values, morals, ethics, principles, and conscience—and still make money!

For more information call 1-800-762-6814

EXCELSIOR VALUE & RESTRUCTURING

The U.S. Trust family has thirty-two funds. This rather oddly named fund was one of seven originally created by

Excelsior in 1993. They targeted demographic trends—such as the aging of the baby boomers—that appeared likely to generate profit. Excelsior Value & Restructuring was the one that hit the jackpot; with 40 percent returns during its first year it beat those for the S&P 500 by 30 points. In the past 5 years it was still beating most equity funds, with returns a shade over 20 percent. Turnover is about 35 percent and expenses are well under 1 percent. If you had invested $10,000 back in early 1993, at inception, it would have grown to about $35,000 in the first five years.

Excelsior Value & Restructuring is the only stock fund focusing solely on this trend. Remarking on its superior performance, *Individual Investor* magazine said, "While some of that success is surely due to the skill of the fund's veteran manager, David J. Williams, part should be attributed to luck. Excelsior threw seven darts and one landed squarely on the bull's eye, focusing on a trend that transformed and boosted countless stocks."

In short, Excelsior rode the tide up as America's large blue-chip companies, facing resistance to price increases and slow sales, have positioned themselves for global competition through such restructuring strategies as cost cutting, layoffs, spin-offs, management changes, mergers, and disposing of unprofitable operations. A staunch value investor, Williams buys companies with solid brands—like IBM, Xerox, and Eastman Kodak—when they're down at 15 or fewer times projected earnings, and he holds them until they reach the current multiple forecast for earnings, about 25 times.

For more information call 1-800-466-1012

FIDELITY DIVIDEND GROWTH

Here's one of the youngsters in Fidelity's family of funds, with a 1993 inception date and a relatively new manager in control. Charles Mangum took control in

1997, although he has been at the helm of a few other Fidelity funds since 1992, having come on board initially as an analyst for medical technology in health care. This no-load fund targets large blue-chip companies with market capitalizations in excess of $5 billion and price-to-earnings ratios in line with those of the S&P 500. In other words, its investment strategy resembles that of an index fund.

The 150 stocks in Dividend Growth's $8 billion portfolio are selected for capital appreciation through steady growth in their dividends. The dominant portfolio sectors are financials, technology, health, and industrial cyclicals. Some of the top holdings include solid brand names like BankAmerica, Citigroup, General Electric, Johnson & Johnson, McKesson, Microsoft, Schering Plough, and Wal-Mart.

The fund's performance has been surprisingly strong despite its relatively short history with a new manager on the job. For example, returns for the most recent 1-year period, as well as 3 and 5 years, are between 25 and 30 percent, which regularly beats the S&P 500. And Mangum is getting these results with a modest expense ratio in the range of 0.85 percent and volatility that's slightly below the S&P 500 benchmark. The fund's turnover is about 110 percent, somewhat above average. If you were lucky enough to invest in this fund at the outset, your $10,000 would now be worth about $40,000, well above the $28,000 growth for the S&P 500.

For more information call 1-800-544-8888

FIDELITY EQUITY-INCOME

Welcome to one of Fidelity's old reliable workhorses, founded in 1966. Its success over the years resulted in Fidelity cloning this $22 billion fund in 1990. Yet, while their investment strategies are quite similar, Equity-Income still manages to outperform its $18 billion younger sibling, Fidelity Equity-Income II. Like other so-called equity-income funds, both are looking for income-producing companies with high current yield, rather than high-growth companies with high valuations. The portfolios of both funds include large positions in household brand names in turnaround positions, such as General Electric, FNMA, Allstate, and American Express. Actually, the size of the fund virtually forces it into the large-cap (companies with market values over $5 billion) arena, using a value-investing style.

Manager Stephen Petersen is a veteran and the fund's chief stock-picker; over three hundred stocks fill out the portfolio of this giant. Petersen joined Fidelity in 1980 and took the helm of Fidelity Equity-Income in 1993. He has survived Fidelity's massive shake-up of managers in recent years, a testament to his strong track record. Over the long term the fund has been a consistently high performer: Total returns were over 20 percent for a recent 3-year period, over 17 percent for 5 years, and about 15 percent for a recent 15-year period. If you had put in $10,000 a decade ago, you'd have over $50,000 today. Petersen and his predecessors have done all this with modest expenses of around two-thirds of a point and turnover around 0.25 percent.

For more information call 1-800-544-8888

FIRST EAGLE FUND OF AMERICA

Jack Schwager, author of the classic *The New Market Wizards,* warns investors: "Do your own thinking. By the time a story is making the cover of the national periodicals, the trend is probably near the end." Schwager would be proud of most value managers, who search for long-term opportunities by scanning huge databases with their sophisticated computer models.

First Eagle managers Harold Levy and David Cohen are true contrarians who just don't fit Schwager's model.

This dynamic duo starts their search in the morning over coffee, scouring the press for hints of turnarounds in undervalued stocks that will jumpstart the companies' recovery: spin-offs, acquisitions, new management, new products, stock repurchases—any signals that suggest a brighter future.

Once their radar locks on a target, Levy and Cohen crank up the computer and begin a disciplined bottom-up analysis, using a cash-flow-to-value criterion. Their unconventional style has worked quite well since inception in 1987; in fact, if you had kicked in $10,000 back then you'd have over $60,000 today. First Eagle manages under half a billion dollars, but judging from their performance, it's likely to grow to much more. With 3-year returns in the 25 percent range, and 10-year performance of about 18 percent, these guys not only are near the top of their peer group, they typically beat the S&P 500 benchmark. Extra! Extra! Read all about it! The Eagle is soaring!

For more information call 1-800-451-3623

GABELLI GROWTH

Back in 1995, Mario Gabelli turned management of the large-cap Gabelli Growth Fund over to Howard Ward, while continuing as manager of his midcap Gabelli Asset Fund. Ward had been a portfolio manager with Scudder before joining Gabelli. The assets of both funds are about $1.1 billion each. In spite of the "Growth" name, Ward maintains a strong allegiance to the Gabelli value-investing style.

Ward scans his blue-chip universe for cheap stocks with strong earnings potential. Typically he finds his bargains in temporarily out-of-favor sectors. His strategy was put to the test immediately after he joined Gabelli in 1995, leading to an increase in the fund's holdings of financial stocks when that sector was down in 1995. He also boosted the fund's tech stocks during the early-1998 dip in that sector. He has now built the sectors to about 20 percent for financials and another 15 percent for technology. With recent 3-year returns hovering around 25 percent and 10-year returns near 20 percent, Ward is certainly upholding the Gabelli value-investing tradition—and going it one better by combining it with the best features of a momentum growth style. In fact, his Gabelli Growth Fund has been outperforming the boss's Gabelli Asset midcap fund. A $10,000 investment in Gabelli Growth 10 years ago would equal about $75,000 today.

For more information call 1-800-422-3554

GABELLI WESTWOOD EQUITY RETAIL

Here's a success story that's guaranteed to get bigger than life in the near future. Portfolio manager Susan Byrne dropped out of college, taught herself Investing 101, and was ignored by the stuffy Wall Street establishment. Rejection led to inspiration: Byrne started her own investment management company in 1983. In 1987 she started the Westwood Equity Fund, and in 1991 she created the Westwood Balanced Fund. Both are relatively small (under a quarter billion dollars each), but that's likely to change in the near future as her tenacity continues to bring "overnight" success.

If success is indeed the best revenge, Byrne has proven her point. She recently merged her management company with Mario Gabelli's operation, entering the upper echelons of the fund world's new ruling powers. The match is a natural, as Byrne's value-oriented approach is a perfect fit with Gabelli's strong roots in the Graham/Dodd tradition. With total returns well over 20 percent for a recent 5-year period, the equity fund shines in the top 5 percent of its category. In fact, if you had put in $10,000 a decade ago you'd have about $50,000 now.

Turnover is usually just under 100 percent, risk is relatively low, and beta is around 0.75. Expenses, however, are somewhat high at 1.50 percent.

Byrne's investment strategy begins with a macroeconomic analysis to isolate sectors and asset allocations. Next, a disciplined bottom-up fundamental analysis is used to pick stocks that are performing much better than market expectations. It's a formula for success that has worked personally and pays off handsomely for her shareholders, too. Bet on this jockey.

For more information call 1-800-937-8966

HARBOR CAPITAL APPRECIATION

With "capital appreciation" in its name, you'd expect this fund to be run by a long-term, buy-and-hold, value-oriented manager, rather than someone driven by earnings growth, as is manager Spiros Segalas. Yet once you get by this oft-repeated lesson in why fund names and labels are so frequently misleading, you'll find Sig Segalas's super-growth fund. The fund has around $3.5 billion in assets and it's climbing, thanks to his outstanding long-term performance record in the large-cap arena. So what if the volatility's a bit high? This fund is first class, with returns of about 20 percent for recent 5- and 10-year periods. An investment of $10,000 a decade ago would be worth over $70,000 today.

What's his secret? Segalas knows how to read the markets and pick growth stocks at a reasonable price. He looks less at the bottom line than at the top line in his bottom-up analysis. He wants to see strong growth in sales, action in new product development, and market dominance, as well as high equity returns and strong balance sheets. Over 75 percent of his portfolio is in four sectors—technology, financial, pharmaceuticals, and services—including market leaders like Microsoft, General Electric, Chase, Dell, Morgan Stanley Dean

Witter, and Walt Disney. Bet on Sig Segalas for long-term capital appreciation driven by growth stocks.

For more information call 1-800-422-1052

JANUS TWENTY

Remember the rule: Bet on the jockey! Well, here's one of our corollaries: Bet on the farm. The Janus family reminds us of Calumet Farms, breeder of eight Kentucky Derby and two Triple Crown winners, including Citation and Whirlaway. Janus had a celebrated jockey in Tom Marsico. When he left in 1997 after a widely publicized rift (and it's rare for a manager to leave Janus), the firm quickly found another hot jockey in its stables, Scott Schoelzel. He was already on board, successfully managing Janus Olympus.

Schoelzel began managing funds at Founders a few years before signing up with Janus in 1994. When he took over the unique Janus Twenty in mid-1997, the fund was already ahead of the others in the field. Like a Pony Express rider, he jumped into the saddle and hasn't looked back since. Janus started Janus Twenty in 1985. After it attracted considerable attention by generating returns of over 50 percent in 1989 and 1991, investors began flocking in. Today the fund has about $10 billion in assets and is still growing.

Janus Twenty is a momentum stock-picker. Unlike the value managers who search for cheap stocks in a slump then wind up holding them for a long period until they recover, a growth stock-picker like Janus Twenty rides hot brand-name blue chips with strong earnings projections. As you might expect, these stocks are pricey, with relatively high price-to-earnings (P/E) ratios; the fund includes such stocks as Dell, Pfizer, and Microsoft. Moreover, as its name implies, it has only a small stable of stocks, usually between twenty and thirty. The name may not be totally accurate, but the strategy works miracles:

$10,000 invested 10 years ago would be worth about $90,000 today. With recent 3-year returns well over 30 percent, this is a hard combination to beat—farm, horse, *and* jockey.

For more information call 1-800-525-8983

LEGG MASON VALUE PRIMARY

Some guys can do no wrong. Or so it seems with manager Bill Miller, who's been running Legg Mason Value Primary since its inception in 1982. Value Primary has the distinction of being the only actively managed stock fund to have beaten the S&P 500 every year since 1991. It's no wonder that a $10,000 investment a decade ago would now be worth around $70,000. As a result of Miller's high-profile success, the fund now manages more than $5 billion in about fifty large-cap stocks, with his top ten holdings equaling about 40 percent of the total.

Miller has a cool, steely-eyed Clint Eastwood style. He knows when to hold and when to fold. He's a classic value-oriented stock-picker. But he also has the uncanny knack of knowing enough to let his winnings ride even when the stocks are on a hot streak and start looking like momentum growth stocks.

Judging from his low turnover (under 20 percent in recent years), Miller doesn't often fold. He's been riding the raging bull market with such winners as Dell, Chase, IBM, America Online, and Citigroup. He's clearly a long-distance runner who's been tested through a few corrections. Hey, it's Miller Time. Place your bets: This guy's a winner.

For more information call 1-800-577-8589

MAIRS & POWER GROWTH

Here's a fund that delivers a powerful message about fund management, especially in an age when there's so much emphasis on asset allocation and, in particular, pressure to diversify internationally. Manager George Mairs is

located within about a twenty-minute drive from many
of the companies in which he invests. Most are in Minnesota, and with just thirty-five companies, Mairs can
easily stay on top of his portfolio.

Contrast that with Mark Mobius, manager of the Templeton Developing Markets fund, with investments
spread all over the globe, in Argentina, Brazil, Hong
Kong, Mexico, Thailand, Turkey, and other remote corners. Mobius virtually lives in his private jet. Maybe one
reason why managers investing outside the United States
have low to modest returns is that they're spread too
thin. Mairs & Powers Growth Fund has been averaging
about 20 percent for the past decade. In fact, if you had
invested $10,000 10 years ago you'd have about $70,000
today. The turnover of this no-load fund is under 5 percent for the past decade, suggesting that they pick solid
domestic companies up front, get to know them, and
hold on to them. That's one very solid track record.

George Mairs may not be living the adventurous and
risky life of a globe-trotting Indiana Jones like Mark
Mobius. But then again, neither are his investors biting
their nails through the jet-lagged rollercoaster ride of
a Templeton Developing Markets Fund. Let Mobius go
hunt for the Temple of Doom. If you're conservative,
and one of the lucky state residents who can invest with
him, bet on Mairs of Minnesota.

For more information call 1-800-304-7404

NEUBERGER & BERMAN PARTNERS

Investors can get a very warm, safe, sleep-peacefully feeling from the Neuberger & Berman family of no-load
funds. It's as if you're at a family gathering, well protected by several uncles the size of NFL linemen. Neuberger & Berman Partners Fund is a large value fund
that's been around since 1968. Ten-year average annual
returns have been in the 15 percent range, close to those

of the S&P 500, as is the fund's beta of 0.90. At approximately 0.80 percent, expenses are below peer-group averages. An investment of $10,000 here a decade ago would have netted you about $50,000 today. The Neuberger family also includes seven other high-caliber funds focused on long-term performance.

Neuberger & Berman Partners' comanager, Robert Gendelman, says that the fund focuses on undervalued situations—stocks selling at discounts. "We think of ourselves as buying pieces of a business, to borrow a phrase from Warren Buffett, and we'd be willing to buy the entire company at the price that we're buying it in the marketplace."

For more information call 1-800-877-9700

NICHOLAS FUND

Do All-American basketball players make All-American fund managers? Well, here's one: Albert Nicholas. Since founding the fund back in 1969, he's built an outstanding long-term track record, averaging over 15 percent for the past 15 years. Son David joined his father as manager of a couple of funds in 1993 and has been comanaging the Nicholas Fund since 1996. In fact, the past few years have been some of the team's best, averaging about 20 percent as the fund's assets have expanded to more than $5 billion. If you'd been lucky enough to have given $10,000 to Nicholas a decade ago, it would have grown to almost $50,000 today.

Albert Nicholas may have been a fast-break king on the basketball court, but his investment style is quite the opposite. A staunch value manager, he picks well at the tip-off. Then he hangs on for a long time, as his 20 percent turnover ratio proves. In addition to the tax efficiency here, returns are enhanced by expenses that are held under 0.75 percent. Like other midcap value funds, Nicholas Fund has a new problem as it morphs into a large-cap growth stock fund, thanks to the sustained bull market. The Nicholas team's stock-picking style has been consistent. They continue with an investment strategy that has worked for three decades by searching for out-of-favor stocks with strong upside earnings potential. Their disciplined and predictable style makes the Nicholas Fund an excellent choice in any individual portfolio.

For more information call 1-800-227-5987

OAKMARK FUND

You can't help feeling your money's in safe hands after talking to Robert Sanborn, manager of the no-load Oakmark Fund, one of the top Growth Fund SuperStars with about $7 billion in total assets. In a day when many fund managers turn over their entire portfolios annually, Sanborn convincingly articulates Oakmark's strategic role: not as a gunslinger who's buying paper stocks in companies that he'll trade at will but more as a hands-on owner, a working partner, or a venture capitalist—someone totally committed for the long haul to the businesses into which he's putting your money.

Turnover hovers around 20 percent, beta is a modest 0.90 percent, expenses are under 1.10 percent, and 3-year returns are close to 20 percent. A $10,000 investment in Oakmark back at inception in 1991 would have been worth over $50,000 7 years later.

My conversation with Sanborn reminded me of my days in the First Marine Air Wing. He has the confidence of a top-gun pilot and the laser precision of a flight engineer. Despite the fund's drop in returns in 1998, he makes you feel that your future's definitely on target with the Oakmark team.

For more information call 1-800-625-6275

PAPP AMERICA-ABROAD

The world economy is undergoing a massive paradigm shift: In 1970 about 67 percent of the capitalization of the global stock market was in the United States. By 1997 it had dropped to 44 percent. Paralleling this shift, many solid American blue chips—such as Exxon, Coca-Cola, General Electric, and Gillette—now generate over 70 percent of their earnings from foreign operations. Also keep in mind that major U.S. companies—like General Electric, with a market capitalization of $273 billion and substantial foreign operations—are bigger than the economies of many foreign countries.

So here's an asset-allocation tip for you: Forget about investing in global and international funds that put your money in little-known foreign companies and high-risk countries. If you really want to invest abroad—for example, if your financial planner or your asset-allocation model "tells" you to diversify internationally—you can fulfill this goal with funds like Papp America-Abroad, which invest only in U.S. blue chips. L. Roy Papp virtually invented this strategy, and with 5-year average annual returns around 20 percent, he's looking like a genius, a patriot, *and* a top-gun manager. These are solid numbers. If you'd given Papp $10,000 back at inception in late 1991, it would have grown to nearly $30,000 in six years.

For more information call 1-800-421-4004

SAFECO EQUITY NO-LOAD

Here's one of the granddaddies of all mutual funds. It's been around since 1932. That's almost seventy years old. Longevity alone deserves our respect, especially when you consider that the vast majority of all mutual funds are less than ten years old. Think of John Glenn going back into space. Fortunately, like Glenn, this fund's got a lot more to offer than mere longevity. It's a top performer as well as a survivor. If you'd plunked down $10,000 10 years ago you'd have watched it grow to about $70,000 today.

The manager of Safeco Equity No-Load, Richard Meagley, makes no bones about it. He's a confirmed long-term buy-and-hold investor, with a portfolio of forty to fifty stocks that he expects to hold for several years. Here are the stats on this large-cap growth fund: Average annualized 10-year returns are about 20 percent; beta, a respectable 0.90; expenses, a low 0.75; and turnover, a low, low 35 percent. Just what you'd expect for a solid, reliable growth fund from a respectable insurer like Safeco Corporation, with its family of nineteen mutual funds.

For more information call 1-800-426-6730

SELECTED AMERICAN SHARES

Here's another wonderful father/son story. Manager Chris Davis inherited his success genes from his father, Shelby Davis, who founded the highly regarded $6 billion Davis New York Venture Fund in 1969. Chris has been working on Shelby's team as a manager since 1993.

Selected American Shares is another real old-timer, one that's been around since 1933. From 1983 to 1992 it was run by another well-known manager, Donald Yacktman, who left to start his own fund. Shelby Davis took command until 1997, when he passed the baton to his son. How's Chris doing with this $2.5 billion fund? Super. He's following in his father's footsteps: In 1997 Selected American Shares not only beat its peer group at 37 percent, it topped the S&P 500 by a few points. You can't get any better than that coming out of the blocks. Moreover, Selected is a no-load, whereas Davis New York Venture has a sizable load. A $10,000 investment a decade ago would be worth about $60,000 today.

True to the Davis value-oriented stock-picking tradition, Selected American Shares is looking for large-cap blue chips being positively affected by broad, long-term, macroeconomic shifts and trends. A heavy (almost 50 percent) weighting in financials—such as American

Express, BankAmerica, Citigroup, Morgan Stanley Dean Witter, and Wells Fargo—has paid off. Fundamentally, Davis wants companies with 15 percent earnings growth selling at P/Es around 10. Like father, like son.

For more information call 1-800-243-1575

SOUND SHORE FUND

They should rename this fund "Safe Shore": You feel your money is well protected traveling with this team. This twelve-year-old midcap value fund with over $1.5 billion in assets is outperforming its peers. The average annual returns—around 20 percent for recent years, with average annual returns over 15 percent for the past decade— make this a winning fund that has been tracking the S&P 500 very closely. A sum of $10,000 invested ten years ago would have risen in value to about $60,000 today.

Sound Shore is guided by a disciplined steady-as-she-goes investment philosophy. Nothing seems to knock them off course. Comanager Gibbs Kane says,

> To a degree that we look at stocks that are unpopular, we're looking at the market at a discount. We're only in stocks where the P/E is about 75 percent of the S&P on consensus earnings for four quarters. And that has been the case almost all of the last twelve years, the life of the fund.
>
> The P/E of the S&P 500 goes up and down, and the P/Es of our stocks go up and down. But we're being hired to find the best names that we can, the best ideas that we can. We're not being hired to give a view of what interest rates are going to do or what foreign corporations or economies are going to do to influence our market. We just don't think that's where our strength lies, and our investors don't think so either.

In the true Maine tradition of frank honesty, they even refer to the fund as dull and boring. Perhaps "safe and sound" is a more accurate description of this fund.

For more information call 1-800-551-1980

T. ROWE PRICE DIVIDEND GROWTH

SmartMoney magazine reported that back about 1991 "only 29 percent of T. Rowe's long-standing equity funds had above-average 5-year records compared with their peer groups, according to Lipper Inc. Today 90 percent of the company's stock funds meet that standard." It was a "revolution from within—they literally taught themselves to be better managers." *SmartMoney* called this "remarkable turnaround" a true "renaissance." Today T. Rowe Price has over seventy funds from which to pick. Started in 1993, the Dividend Growth Fund is one of the many products of this transformation.

Manager William Stromberg has been running the show since the start, and if you were there back then with $10,000 it would have grown to almost $30,000 in the first six years. Stromberg is very aware that this is a "dividend-growth" fund: At least 65 percent of his holdings are companies with solid, proven records of above-average earnings and increasing dividend growth, strong balance sheets, and capital appreciation. Turnover was about 40 percent recently. This $1 billion-plus fund plays it safe, with volatility (beta of 0.65) lower than that of the S&P 500, while at the same time generating better than 22 percent returns that come close to matching those of the S&P 500 in the past five years.

For more information call 1-800-638-5660

T. ROWE PRICE EQUITY-INCOME

If you were to build a one-fund portfolio—or if you're a new investor just starting out and looking for your first fund—here's a top candidate, rivaling T. Rowe Price's Dividend Growth Fund. It's solid and conservative, with no loads and no nonsense. Manager Brian C. Rogers has been at the helm since 1985. If you'd bought in when he started, you'd have almost $10 for every $1 you invested back then. Rogers targets undervalued large-cap companies that are poised to turn up in the near future, with 80 percent of his assets in name-brand S&P 500 companies like General Electric, Atlantic Richfield, Exxon, and Chase Manhattan. You'll sleep peacefully with this fund.

Performance is high while risk is low. As Rogers once told *Money* magazine, "I've found that most investors don't want as much risk as they say they do." Average returns are 15 percent for the past decade, and $10,000 invested a decade ago would now be worth about $50,000. Turnover is only 25 percent. Volatility is less than two-thirds that of the market. And expenses are a mere 0.80 percent, compared with the stock fund average of 1.40 percent.

If there is a perfect all-American fund, this one fits the profile. With funds like this around, you might easily forget about investing with the new fund supermarkets and stay with just one large mutual fund family. After all, T. Rowe Price has over seventy funds from which to choose and a tradition of picking managers like Brian Rogers.

For more information call 1-800-638-5660

T. ROWE PRICE MID-CAP GROWTH

Here's another winner from the T. Rowe Price family of funds, started in 1992 on the leading edge of their "renaissance," as *SmartMoney* called the company's turnaround. Manager Brian Berghuis was one of the first managers of a midcap fund, investing in companies with between $1 billion and $5 billion in assets. He's been on board since the fund came out of the gate in 1992. Since then he's created a solid performer with over $2.5 billion in assets invested 65 percent in midcaps with high growth potential. Now he's at the top of his game, resting in the top 5 percent of his peer group for the past five years, while enjoying low risk compared with his peers. A $10,000 investment here would have grown to almost $35,000 in the first six years.

Like so many other T. Rowe Price funds, this one follows the founder's edict: "It's not timing the market, it's time in the market." Berghuis is steering Mid-Cap down a conservative road compared with its peers; indeed, he'll take it as a compliment if you call his portfolio boring. He pursues no aggressive moves, no hot stocks, no big-time momentum plays—just solid, long-term capital appreciation. Find companies whose valuations are down, bet on the recovery with projected earnings growth of 15 percent or better within 3 to 5 years, stay away from high P/E ratios, and you wind up with a midcap fund that's a peer-group-beater.

For more information call 1-800-638-5660

TORRAY FUND

Robert E. Torray is a classic value investor, with absolute confidence in himself. When asked what percentage of an investor's portfolio ought to be allocated to his fund, he replied with total confidence and without hesitation, "I think it ought to be 100 percent"—and that may not be such a bad idea. His average returns were about 25 percent in recent years, and turnover was less than 20 percent. If you'd invested $10,000 with Torray at the inception of his fund in 1990, you'd have over $40,000 today, matching the return on the S&P 500. As Torray himself put it,

> We only look for two or three investments a year. And if we find five, we'll buy five. Our approach is substantially reactive. We just wait until we observe in a company or an industry falling share prices, and that triggers a research effort. I've been in the business thirty-five years. I'm generally familiar with how various industries and businesses operate, how they interrelate to each other. So it's not a major thing for me and our company to see a falling share price and be able to assess a situation pretty rapidly. We're in a position to invest in some businesses if we studied them

for a day. Others, like AT&T, we studied and thought about for three years, during which time the stock went sideways and down.

With that kind of discipline it's easy to understand why he's a winning jockey.

For more information call 1-800-443-3036

VANGUARD GROWTH & INCOME

Vanguard is the king of index funds. They pride themselves on being penny-pinching tightwads, cutting corners everywhere to save a few hundredths of a basis point for their fund owners. Of course, their index funds are designed to beat the competition by forcing them into a handicap race: What else would you call it when their average index fund expenses are around 0.20 percent versus 1.40 percent for the average stock fund?

So why would the Vanguard family welcome John Nagorniak's odd-ball Growth & Income Fund—a $4 billion, large-cap, enhanced-index fund whose avowed goal is to beat the index? After all, if he succeeds, wouldn't it embarrass Vanguard's straight-laced index funds by beating them? Maybe it was a sense of adventure in this otherwise ultraconservative family of funds. Or perhaps a shrewd move by Vanguard's founder John Bogle to create some good-natured in-house competition and keep the rest of the team on their toes.

Nagorniak has been at the helm since 1986 and he does hit the target regularly. How? That's the secret of the enhanced-index fund approach. He clones the S&P 500 with 65 percent of your money, then cleverly positions the rest in value-oriented positions, slightly overweighted in the tech sector. The rest of the fund, however, is solidly locked into the core index companies. Still, their beta is only slightly higher than that of the S&P 500, and their expenses are typically Vanguard: less than 0.40 percent in spite of the active-management component. With 10-year returns close to 20 percent, this one's a winner, like its older and bigger sibling, Vanguard U.S. Growth. If you'd had $10,000 in Vanguard's Growth & Income (or U.S. Growth) for the past 10 years, you'd have over $60,000 today.

For more information call 1-800-662-7447

VANGUARD WINDSOR II

Yes, the original large-cap Vanguard Windsor Fund is still around, and has been since 1958, with over $20 billion in assets. The fund was so successful it had to close the doors to new investors. Then Windsor II came out of the gate in 1985 and now has over $30 billion under management. Not long ago *Money* magazine called Windsor II a "fund to buy now and hold forever." Expenses are very low (under 0.40 percent and about half those of its peer group), giving Windsor II a clear lead over the competition.

The fund's lead manager, James Barrows, has been holding down the fort since inception in the mid-1980s, so he's earned his stripes as a hardened veteran of a few bearish corrections. Turnover hovers below 30 percent in his search for long-term values. Barrows recently outlined his three guiding rules for picking stocks in *Worth* magazine: (1) Buy stocks trading at 25 to 35 percent of the S&P 500 average; (2) the stocks must be trading at a price/book ratio two-thirds the benchmark; and (3) yield should be 150 percent of the index.

With over 250 stocks in the portfolio, is it too unwieldy? Hardly. Barrows got some help, not only from the in-house team but also from three different outside management companies, each separately managing 10 percent of the assets. Although you'd better not expect much current income from this kind of portfolio, Windsor II has tracked the S&P 500 within a hair for most of the last decade. A $10,000 investment in Windsor II a decade ago would now be worth about $60,000. If past performance counts for anything, you probably *can* buy this fund and hold it forever.

For more information call 1-800-662-7447

WHITE OAK GROWTH STOCK

Thank God: Here's a genuine breath of fresh air, a stock fund that isn't slowly morphing into an index fund. In today's competitive world, fund managers are forced to mimic their benchmarks—so much so that they eventually turn their funds into virtual index clones.

Not so with Jim Oelschlager. Hardly a newcomer, he started the White Oak Fund in 1992 after years of honing his skills managing billions for large institutions. Oelschlager's unique strategy narrowly targets just three high-growth sectors, which he selects based on macroeconomic trends. Currently these are financial, technology, and health care. From there on it's a fundamental search for growth at a reasonable price. Like Warren Buffett, he's focused on a few great companies in building a concentrated portfolio of just twenty-five stocks, with names like Cisco, Compaq, Sun, Oracle, and Microsoft.

As the White Oak Growth Stock Fund begins to catch the eye of the investing public, expect it to grow into a mighty oak, reaching the $1 billion range. Why? After a shaky start in 1993 and 1994, Oelschlager hit his stride in 1995 with an incredible 52 percent total return, 15 points above the S&P 500. Three-year returns are in the 25 percent range. A $10,000 investment would have netted you about $35,000 in the first 6 years. Although the ride's a bit more volatile than that for the majority of large-cap growth funds, his contrarian strategy is working magic. Like Frank Sinatra, he's doing it his way. Oelschlager is "#1 with a bullet"—a hit record moving up the charts!

For more information call 1-800-462-5386

Aggressive-Growth, Small-Cap, and Capital-Appreciation Funds

THE FUNDS CONSIDERED here typically aim for high returns from capital appreciation rather than income or dividend growth. They also take greater risks than most of the funds discussed in the previous section. For example, they may invest in microcap companies, out-of-favor industries, options, derivatives, and leveraging. The fund managers are typically actively managing and trading their assets, with high turnover ratios and higher than average expenses. Academic gurus theorize that higher returns follow such higher risks.

Volatility can be 15 to 40 percent higher than that of the stock market as a whole, making these funds less appropriate for the most conservative investors. Moreover, research shows that the average long-term return for aggressive growth funds is only about 1 percent higher than the returns for growth funds: 11.6 percent versus 10.4 percent. Such scant improvement in returns may not be worth the extra risks for investors with a less aggressive perspective or immediate needs.

Some experts recommend that you allocate 25 percent of your portfolio to these funds, provided that you are prepared for the added anxiety and have a long time horizon for the investments. Understandably, many investors tend to be more conservative, so 5 to 15 percent may be fine for them. Anyone with a 5-year or shorter time frame—in particular a conservative, risk-

```
┌─────────────────────────────────────────────────┐
│  ███████ SUPERSTAR STOCK FUNDS ███████           │
│                                                   │
│  AGGRESSIVE-GROWTH, SMALL-CAP, AND CAPITAL-APPRECIATION │
│   1  Acorn Fund                                   │
│   2  Baron Asset                                  │
│   3  Eclipse Equity                               │
│   4  Managers Special Equity                      │
│   5  Safeco Growth No-Load                        │
│   6  T. Rowe Price New American Growth            │
│   7  T. Rowe Price Small-Cap Stock                │
│   8  Third Avenue Value                           │
│   9  Tweedy, Browne American Value                │
│  10  Rydex Nova                                   │
└─────────────────────────────────────────────────┘
```

averse investor—should consider staying out of aggressive growth and small-cap funds altogether.

But if you are prepared for a wild ride, these funds can make you money. Here's the elite group of leading funds.

ACORN FUND

His book has a delightfully whimsical title, *A Zebra in Lion Country;* his face, the impish smile of an Irish leprechaun; his humor, reminiscent of Will Rogers's best. The book is aptly subtitled *Ralph Wanger's Investment Survival Guide.* But *survival?* This guy has done a lot better than survive. He's a living legend. When he tells you the best way to pick a mutual fund is alphabetically, he's right and he can prove it. His Acorn Fund is one of the best gosh-darn small-caps around, managing over $3 billion in assets.

On pure stats, Wanger's a consistent winner: His fund has been around since he started it in 1970. He runs a tight ship. Expenses are low: under 0.60 percent. Turnover is low: 32 percent. Beta is low: around 0.90. And he's widely diversified in three hundred stocks. Net result:

Acorn's returns are near the top of the small caps. In fact, if you invested in Acorn a decade ago, you'd be thanking the gods for the $50,000 you have today.

What's his secret to success? Like Will Rogers, his home-spun tales make it all seem so easy. He calls his value-investing style GAARP, for "Growth At A Reasonable Price." And Wanger says he avoids the highly volatile and risky high-tech sector by going "downstream from technology" for opportunities among low-tech suppliers and users. That may sound more like a tracker on the Serengeti Plain than an ace portfolio manager talking, but it all works. So if your portfolio's heading into lion country, bet on the zebra.

For more information call 1-800-922-6769

BARON ASSET

What do nursing homes, bowling alleys, radio stations, and orange juice have in common? How about the future of America—and the Baron Asset Fund. Baron Asset Fund is one of the funds in the top aggressive-growth, small-cap category. Working within broad cultural and economic "megatrends," the Baron Asset team uses a value-oriented strategy to identify companies that are successfully riding these long-term megatrends.

Ron Baron's team has done a remarkable job since starting this fund just prior to the crash of 1987. Returns have averaged close to 15 percent for the past ten years. Risk is low, with beta about 1.10. And while expenses are about average, turnover hovers around 15 percent, making the Baron funds extremely tax-efficient.

As Morty Schaja, chief operating officer of the Baron management team, says, "We're partners with the management teams, as opposed to a trader. So we're really analyzing their strategies and the opportunities that an individual company has. We call that 'bottom-up.' If we find companies that will double in size for the next four or five years, then in a good market we'll make 120 percent. And in a bad market, we'll make 80 percent. But if we're right about the underlying businesses that we're investing in, we'll do fine in a good market and in a bad market." Good market, bad market, doesn't matter. If you invested $10,000 with Baron Asset ten years ago, you'd be sitting pretty with over $55,000 today.

For more information call 1-800-992-2766

ECLIPSE EQUITY

Remember the quiet math whiz in school who never seemed to do any fun stuff and always got the high grades? Eclipse Equity reminds me of him: nose to the grindstone, disciplined, meticulous. They've been around since just before the crash in 1987 and currently manage about $200 million spread across about three hundred assets— about the same number as Acorn, which is over 25 times bigger. Wesley McCain has been in charge for the whole trip, with Kathy O'Connor joining him as comanager in 1990.

They are classic value-oriented stock-pickers. Their strategy relies heavily on a purely quantitative model to screen and rank their database of six thousand stocks and pick undervalued names that are also showing signs of turnaround that will lead to growth in earnings and asset value. In short, the McCain-O'Connor management team is looking for the best of both worlds: value plus upside growth. And they're getting it.

Recent performance has lagged slightly. But still, with 3- and 10-year returns around 15 percent, their record is excellent against that of the small-cap competition. In fact, they not only beat their small-cap peers, they beat their benchmark index. A $10,000 investment a decade ago would be valued at about $40,000 today. Eclipse Equity is a solid choice.

For more information call 1-800-872-2710

MANAGERS SPECIAL EQUITY

Here's a new twist on diversification: Four managers each independently run a quarter of the fund's $1 billion in assets. In effect, you're diversifying across four separate small-cap funds for the price of one. The fund was started in 1984, but most of the current management team came on board in 1994.

The managers include Gary Pilgrim, with a momentum style; Andrew Knuth, adopting a value approach to small caps; and Tim Ebright and Robert Kern in a value-based search for promising microcaps. It sounds like Notre Dame's famed Four Horsemen, or the Modern Jazz Quartet. And, yes, this team of stars performs quite well together.

Here's their scorecard: Turnover is a modest 50 percent. Volatility equals the peer group average. Expenses hover under 1.40 percent. And their longer-term returns are just over 15 percent, typically several points over the Russell 2000 benchmark. A $10,000 investment here a decade ago would be worth about $50,000 today. This investment strategy may seem strange at first, but you sure can't argue with their performance. Managers Special Equity has consistently been one of the best in the small-cap category.

For more information call 1-800-835-3879

SAFECO GROWTH NO-LOAD

If you thought the S&P 500 was hot in 1997 with 33.4 percent returns, here's an oddball small-cap fund that topped out at 50 percent. No wonder the cash started flowing in until it's now at about $1.5 billion. But before you jump in, remember: This fund is run by humans subject to the whims of the market. It also had negative returns in 1990, 1992, and 1994. Still, it's an excellent investment for a long-term, risk-tolerant investor.

Why is it so successful? Simply because its long-term returns also consistently beat those of its small-cap competition: The fund's recent 3-year average was well over 20 percent, about double that of the benchmark Russell 2000, and returns were a shade over 15 percent for the past decade. This is definitely a successful long-distance runner, turning the $10,000 investment of a decade ago into about $50,000 today.

Manager Thomas Maguire has been running funds for Safeco since 1984, about the time Safeco Growth opened its doors. He took command of this fund in 1989. His style baffles analysts and financial journalists alike. Here's how he put it to *Kiplinger's:* "I buy small-cap, midcap, large-cap, whatever. I like to invest in stocks that go up." And up they go. For solid long-term capital appreciation, it pays to bet on a manager with a track record like Maguire's.

For more information call 1-800-426-6730

T. ROWE PRICE NEW AMERICAN GROWTH

Here's another top-performing growth fund from the T. Rowe Price family of funds, started in 1985 before the firm's "renaissance" of the 1990s, as *SmartMoney* called its turnaround. New American Growth is another, more aggressive, midcap fund comanaged by John Laporte and Brian Berghuis, who also manages T. Rowe Price's Mid-Cap Growth Fund.

Their success comes from picking low-profile stocks. These managers have minimized their holdings in the high-flying tech stocks and put their money into less-volatile, steady performers in the services sectors—companies in health care, retail, media, telecommunications, financial, and business services that have profited from the economic growth of the 1990s. Interestingly, one of their key holdings has been Franklin Resources, manager of one of the ten largest fund families and a competitor.

Over the years this $1.5 billion fund has grown from a small-cap to a midcap to a large-cap fund, due in part to the incredible bull market, as well as the managers' solid picks. Turnover is about 80 percent, with beta in line with that of the benchmark S&P 500. Ten-year returns are close to 15 percent, ranking second in the top 10 percent of the fun's peer group and making New American Growth a solid, proven pick for any portfolio. Had you put $10,000 into this fund a decade ago you'd have about $50,000 today.

For more information call 1-800-426-6730

T. ROWE PRICE SMALL-CAP STOCK

This is another strong fund from the ever-conservative T. Rowe Price family. Their Small-Cap Stock Fund began accepting investors in 1988, and the fund has done very well since Greg McCrickard took charge in 1992. The investment strategy is an eclectic blend of value and growth, although the portfolio as a whole tilts more toward a value orientation. This best-of-both-worlds approach to portfolio management scans the horizon for solid companies with low valuations, a turnaround catalyst in progress, and the strong prospect of earnings growth. Its track record has helped propel the fund to about $1 billion in assets, broadly diversified into more than two hundred stocks.

McCrickard's Small-Cap Stock Fund has consistently beat the small-cap benchmark, the Russell 2000, over the past 3- and 5-year periods, with just under 15 percent returns. Although returns were down in 1998, a $10,000 investment of a decade ago would now be worth about $40,000. Perhaps even more important for conservative investors looking for a solid small-cap to round out their portfolios, this one carries about half the volatility of the S&P 500. The turnover ratio is normally less than 0.25, and expenses are modest (in the 1.00 percent range).

The McCrickard–T. Rowe Price combo is definitely a first-class act.

For more information call 1-800-638-5660

THIRD AVENUE VALUE

Third Avenue Value is a no-load aggressive-growth fund with $1.5 billion under management. The results speak for themselves. Turnover: under 15 percent; beta: below average at 0.70; expenses: 1.10 percent. In addition, 3-year returns have topped 15 percent, making this a peer group–beater, especially when you discover that $10,000 invested here would have been worth over $40,000 just 8 years later.

Interviewing Martin Whitman, the manager, was a rare learning experience: like sitting in on one of his finance classes at Yale University; like soaking up the wisdom of a gentle, centered Zen master; like touring Manhattan with a salty cab driver. He's the classic value investor, one who applies his approach with the iron-willed conviction of a Samurai warrior . . . targeted, disciplined, unwavering.

Whitman builds a "safe" portfolio using his four criteria for value investing: (1) The most important criterion is that the company have an exceptionally strong financial position. (2) It must be reasonably managed from a stockholder point of view. (3) It must be in a business Whitman understands. (4) It must be "cheap": He tries not to pay more than fifty cents for every dollar he thinks the company might be worth, as a private company or in a takeover. So far, Marty is safely in the top half of his peer group.

For more information call 1-800-443-1021

TWEEDY, BROWNE AMERICAN VALUE

What is "value" investing? How does it differ from "growth" investing? Tweedy, Browne knows. They are classic "value" managers, direct descendants of the Graham/

Dodd tradition. Tweedy, Browne's $1 billion American Value Fund is a top-ten stock fund SuperStar: low, low turnover under 10 percent, beta around 0.75, and 3-year returns around 25 percent. In its first 5 years, a $10,000 investment would have grown to about $25,000. Why is this fund so successful? To begin with, Ben Graham and Warren Buffett were Tweedy, Browne's mentors. We asked their managers, Christopher H. Browne and John D. Spears, how the Graham/Dodd tradition became part of the Tweedy, Browne investment philosophy:

> Ben Graham is called the Father of Securities Analysis. He was a professor of investments at Columbia Business School in the 1930s, and coauthor of the first textbook on securities analysis with David Dodd, interestingly enough called *Securities Analysis.* Graham wrote a second book for the layman called *The Intelligent Investor.* His basic thesis was that there are two values to every share of stock: (1) There's the last price at which the shares traded, and (2) then there's the value that would be received in the event that the company was sold in an arms-length negotiated transaction between a knowledgeable buyer and a knowledgeable seller. That's what he called intrinsic value.

One of Graham's key pupils subsequently became a partner in Tweedy, Browne and brought with him Graham's value-investing strategy, which remains the cornerstone of their success.

For more information call 1-800-432-4789

RYDEX NOVA

Modern portfolio theory says that the higher the risk, the greater the potential return. Here's a perfect example of that principle in the aggressive-growth category. If you still believe the forecasts of a 20-year global economic boom, or if you're convinced that the bull market will continue in full force—and even go higher, possibly exceeding 20,000 by 2010—this is the fund for you. Rydex Nova's goal is a high 1.50 beta to the S&P 500. So if the market index goes up 30 percent, the fund should go up 45 percent.

Surprisingly, it has come close to its goal since opening its doors in 1993. The returns have been phenomenal, averaging almost 30 percent annually in a recent 3-year period. Since moving sideways in a sideways market in 1994, a $10,000 investment in Nova would have tripled to $30,000 in the few years between 1995 to 1998.

This unusual fund invests over $600 million in the risky futures and options market, so you should expect a lot more volatility and risk in pursuit of higher returns. Let's be frank: It's primarily a fund for very sophisticated professional money managers. But the fact is that Rydex Nova is also becoming popular with a new breed of street-smart individual do-it-yourself investors, perhaps explaining why it was so frequently recommended on the 150 "best-funds" lists we monitor.

Nevertheless, Rydex Nova is *not* for the average investor. Morningstar cautions: "Fund traders usually have lousy timing. Morningstar research indicates that investors who move in and out of funds usually garner lower returns than could be had with a simple strategy of dollar cost averaging."

Remember, Nova is purposely designed to be 50 percent *more volatile* than the S&P 500, so what goes up big goes down big. Still, you should study Nova: Understand why it won't work for you, or why it will. And if you're a long-term, buy-and-hold investor, find out why Nova is a favorite among short-term market timers.

For more information call 1-800-820-0888

Global and International Funds

HERE WE CONSIDER FUNDS that invest in foreign companies, markets, and economies. This category includes global, international, foreign, and world funds. They may also invest in domestic companies with substantial revenues from foreign trade; in foreign companies investing in the United States; and in developed countries, emerging markets, and single-country funds, which are higher-risk investments. Assets often include equities and debt, both government and corporate securities. Generally speaking, we recommend that the average investor focus on developed countries and/or domestic companies generating substantial revenues from foreign operations, in order to minimize portfolio risks and maximize potential returns.

FOREIGN INTRIGUE

ONLY A THIRD OF ALL individuals invest in funds specializing in foreign investments, despite the fact that most professional planners recommend diversifying part of your portfolio overseas. Apparently most investors are still trying to get over that initial hurdle about whether or not they should invest overseas, especially with the sustained global crisis of recent years.

Considering the widespread global economic turmoil rippling throughout the world—forcefully in Asia, Russia, and Latin America—in recent times, you'll see that these particular global funds have held up quite well. The reasons they've done so well can be summarized in the following three rules for investing overseas:

GLOBAL RULE #1: STICK TO THE DEVELOPED ECONOMIES

Janus Worldwide is an excellent example of the elements that make for a winning fund as Asia and other emerging nations recover from the corrections of recent years. It offers proof that if you insist on investing overseas, it makes sense to stick with funds that invest in the developed nations, particularly in Europe.

When the Asian correction hit in 1997, Janus Worldwide had over 65 percent of its stock holdings in developed nations in Europe, and only 3 percent in Pacific Rim countries outside Japan:

- United Kingdom   12.6%
- Germany   11.3%
- Switzerland   11.2%
- United States   10.0%
- France   9.0%
- Netherlands   8.8%
- Sweden   7.0%
- Japan   6.8%
- Italy   2.7%
- Finland   2.2%

The 3-year returns by country varied only about 1 percent as a result of the Hong Kong Flu.

Of course, buying into a global fund that invests primarily in developed economies is no guarantee of relatively stable returns. Vanguard International Growth, a 16-year-old fund, had 50 percent of its holdings in Europe and over 40 percent in Japan and Pacific Rim countries; it saw its returns drop about 5 points after the Asian correction.

As a general rule, however, buying funds that invest in developed nations is a safer bet. Better yet, diversify by investing in a fund that invests across several countries in, for example, Europe rather than in one country. Or diversify even more broadly with a fund like Janus Worldwide.

GLOBAL RULE #2: AVOID EMERGING-MARKET FUNDS

Conversely, here's the geographic distribution of returns for one of the hardest hit of the global funds on our radar screen during the Asia crisis—Montgomery Emerging Markets, a 5-year-old fund that invests in higher-risk economies:

◆ Brazil	9.3%
◆ Malaysia	9.0%
◆ Taiwan	8.3%
◆ Hong Kong	6.8%
◆ Russia	5.7%
◆ South Africa	5.6%
◆ India	4.4%
◆ Philippines	4.0%
◆ Portugal	3.9%
◆ South Korea	3.6%

Montgomery Emerging Markets had been a favorite of many leading financial publications. Back in 1993, its second year of operation, it enjoyed a fabulous 58.7 percent return, followed by negative returns in both 1994 and 1995, and a positive 12.3 percent return in 1996. After the correction its 3-year returns turned negative. Unfortunately, such extreme volatility must be expected if you decide to invest in a high-risk, emerging-market fund.

Rule #2 is the corollary to Rule #1: stay out of emerging-market funds unless you have an extremely long view plus a high tolerance for risk and the anxieties that follow in the wake of high volatility.

People who invest in emerging-market funds should be playing with money they can afford to lose, not their living expenses or retirement money. Vegas slot machines, Broadway plays, and an Irish Sweepstakes ticket are comparable investments. If you just want quick fixes and cheap thrills, take up skydiving or bungee jumping. The drops are even faster, and they're cheaper as well.

GLOBAL RULE #3: BUY ONLY DOMESTIC U.S. FUNDS INVESTING IN COMPANIES WITH SIZABLE FOREIGN TRADE

The high-priced "spin doctors" hired by fund managers may have been manipulating you into believing that it is essential that your portfolio have some money overseas in order to diversify adequately.

The reality is that with $5.5 trillion in the single largest capitalized mutual fund market in the world, you can probably find all the diversification you need with a proper allocation of domestic funds, picking large-cap, blue-chip U.S. growth funds.

Perhaps one of the best proponents of this idea is Gary Brinson, one of the leading researchers on the importance of asset allocation over specific selection of stocks and funds. Brinson, now principal manager of more than $350 billion for the Union Bank of Switzerland, had this to say about global investing: "It has become difficult for me to distinguish within this global market between countries. Coca-Cola is a great example. It generates 80 percent of its profits outside the United States. Nestlé, a Swiss company, generates 43 percent of its profits inside the United States. Which is more of a U.S. company? Over the next 10 years, it will not be useful to talk companies and sectors of one vast global equity market, and we'll look at performance in that vein."

In fact, here are the largest U.S. companies ranked by foreign revenues in billions, along with the percentage of their total revenues derived from foreign sources, according to *Forbes:*

- Exxon $92.5 (77%)
- General Motors $51.0 (29%)
- Ford Motor $47.0 (32%)
- IBM $45.8 (58%)
- Mobil $35.6 (60%)

- Texaco $33.4 (56%)
- General Electric $27.0 (30%)
- Hewlett-Packard $23.8 (56%)
- Chevron $23.0 (47%)
- Citicorp $21.6 (62%)

Whatever you do, don't give up on global funds. Despite the short-term reality check of recent years, as John Naisbitt said in *Megatrends Asia,* "The 21st Century belongs to Asia." Moreover, over 55 percent of the world's market capitalization is now outside the United States, and that percentage will grow even larger in the next century. So when you're planning your portfolio, keep in mind that a well-diversified portfolio will typically have somewhere between 5 and 10 percent of its assets overseas, although over the long term U.S. stock funds beat European stock funds 16 percent to 13 percent. The new Euro and the European Monetary Union may change all that, however.

TOP-TEN GLOBAL SUPERSTARS: A MILD CASE OF THE FLU, THEN RIGHT BACK TO WORK!

MOST OF THE Global SuperStars have solid 3-year track records. Many have also been around 5 to 10 years or more. This Global SuperStar Funds list includes top performers traditionally classified as global (both foreign and domestic companies) and international (investing only in foreign companies). Since the portfolios of most individual investors are likely to include just one or at the most two of these global funds anyway, higher-risk overseas funds—such as emerging-market funds, single-country funds, and high-yield overseas debt funds—have been screened out.

Here are the top-ten Global SuperStars:

TOP GLOBAL AND INTERNATIONAL SUPERSTAR FUNDS

1 Brinson Global
2 BT Investment International Equity
3 Fidelity Diversified International
4 Hotchkis & Wiley International
5 Invesco European
6 Janus Worldwide
7 T. Rowe Price European Stock
8 Tweedy Browne Global Value
9 Scudder Global
10 USAA International

BRINSON GLOBAL

Gary Brinson is more than a fund manager; he's an icon. He's been at the forefront of several megatrends in the financial world: He was an asset-allocation pioneer, a portfolio management theorist, a high-tech quantitative analyst, a global-investment strategist—in short, a renaissance man. No wonder Union Bank of Switzerland recently acquired his firm. Today, UBS Brinson is managing $350 billion in institutional assets for the bank.

The Brinson Global Fund was started in 1992 and now manages around $600 million in assets. His much smaller Global Equity Fund was started in 1994. Like other successful global funds, Brinson Global has about 75 percent in the developed nations of Europe and the United States and very little in the riskier Asian markets. But take a closer look and you'll see evidence of a distinctly different strategy. With about 40 percent of its holdings in bonds, this is actually a classic asset-allocation hybrid.

Why? Brinson is an avowed bear. He believes the next decade will see U.S. stocks returning only 7 percent, equal to bond returns but without their safety. His portfolio strategy reflects this forecast: little downside risk with value-oriented stocks and a large bond segment. Nevertheless, in a recent 3-year period Global returned an average of roughly 12 percent annually, with relatively low volatility and risk. A $10,000 investment here would have grown to just under $20,000 in the 5 years after its start-up. This fund may be ideal for risk-averse investors looking for conservative international funds in their portfolios.

For more information call 1-800-448-2430

BT INVESTMENT INTERNATIONAL EQUITY

The Bankers Trust family of funds has done well with this foreign stock fund since its inception in 1992. This $1.5 billion-plus portfolio is managed by a team that took control in 1993 and 1994, including Michael Levy and Robert Reiner. The fund invests only in companies outside the United States.

Their secret to success is actually quite simple. Although the fund had the option of investing in emerging nations, Levy and Reiner have narrowly focused on the developed nations of Europe, with a strategy heavily weighted in financial stocks. That approach has kept them out of trouble. With only 10 percent of its assets allocated to Japan and the Pacific Rim, BT International managed to avoid the impact of the Asian crisis.

Even more important, the fund has also outperformed its European peers with 3- to 5-year average annual returns of 17 percent, almost twice those of the Morgan Stanley world stock index (MSCI EAFE). A $10,000 investment in this fund at inception would have grown to more than $25,000 in the first 5 years. This performance is being achieved by taking positions in companies located in secondary European markets, such as Ireland and Italy. Now, with the new European Monetary

Union in place, the future is likely to continue extremely bullish for this fund.

For more information call 1-800-730-1313

FIDELITY DIVERSIFIED INTERNATIONAL

Greg Fraiser began managing portfolios at Fidelity in 1989 and took charge of Diversified International in 1991. This fund manages over $2 billion in assets, investing in companies with $100 million-plus capitalizations. Fraiser is certainly making sure that the fund lives up to its name: It is diversified across more than seven hundred stocks, with strong positions in financials, industrial cyclicals, and the service industries. Fortunately, the Japan and the Pacific Rim stocks accounted for less than 20 percent of its assets during the Asia crisis.

Fraiser's portfolio-building strategy uses two computer models of the macro- and microdynamics of world markets: one a system for allocating assets top-down among countries, and the other a bottom-up model for picking value-oriented stocks using the usual fundamental benchmarks. Portfolio turnover hovers under 100 percent and expenses are about average at 1.25 percent.

You can't knock success. Some think Fraiser's portfolio is too big. Some say he's too willing to let subjective factors—like politics and economics—override the models. But the bottom line is that Fraiser's portfolio strategy works. In recent years, Diversified International beat its peer index, with total returns over 15 percent. A $10,000 investment at inception would have grown to over $20,000 in 6 years.

For more information call 1-800-544-8888

HOTCHKIS & WILEY INTERNATIONAL

Back in 1970, 67 percent of the market capitalization of the world was in the United States; by 1997 it was only 45 percent. That's a huge shift. Think of it this way: More than 55 percent of today's opportunities for wealth building are now outside the United States, and these world economies are growing rapidly.

Most asset-allocation models tend to recommend nondomestic investments in the range of 5 percent, to a maximum of perhaps 25 percent for an aggressive portfolio. Sarah H. Ketterer is a relatively conservative value-oriented fund manager who is confident enough about the world markets to recommend 30 percent for a long-term buy-and-hold investor. Why? She is convinced that the opportunities really are that strong throughout the world.

Ketterer comanages the Hotchkis & Wiley International Fund as well as the Hotchkis & Wiley Global Equity Fund. Hotchkis & Wiley is a family of nine funds—including balanced, equity-income, mid-cap, small-cap, corporate bond, and total return funds—giving their investors enough choices to build a complete portfolio within this classy, one-stop shop.

Hotchkis & Wiley International invests only in the blue-chip companies of developed countries, using a value-oriented strategy to generate average returns of about 10 percent for the past 5 years. Expenses are well below those of their peers at 0.90 percent. Turnover is a conservative 20 percent. And volatility is well below the S&P 500 benchmark, with a beta around 0.65. A $10,000 investment here would have grown to more than $25,000 in the 7 years since the fund's inception in 1990.

For more information call 1-800-346-7301

INVESCO EUROPEAN
The Invesco family of funds created this foreign stock fund in 1986. Steve Chamberlain took charge in 1990 and built it into a winning portfolio. In 1998 a management team took over the responsibilities. Under Chamberlain's leadership Invesco European, with around $700 million in assets, has outpaced its peer-group rivals with returns

over 25 percent in recent years. In fact, $10,000 invested a decade ago would be worth about $35,000 today.

Chamberlain's strategy capitalized on the tremendous economic growth in the developed nations of Europe in the 1990s. In recent years, about two-thirds of his portfolio was invested in three sectors: financial services, telecommunications, and technology stocks. Within those targeted sectors, his stock-picking focused on companies with solid fundamentals, growing earnings, and strong balance sheets. With the economic consolidation of the European nations, the future looks very optimistic. This fund should continue as a high performer.

For more information call 1-800-525-8085

JANUS WORLDWIDE

Janus is one of the world's leading no-load fund families, and their Janus Worldwide fund is the pick of the litter. Helen Young Hayes has been with Janus since 1987. In 1992 she became the lead manager of Janus Worldwide, taking over the reins of a small $200 million fund from James Craig, the manager of the flagship Janus Fund. Today the fund has become enormously successful and popular with investors, so Hayes has had her hands full with over $15 billion in assets pouring in.

Janus Worldwide invests in foreign and domestic companies, typically large-cap brand names with strong earnings growth potential. Global economic trends play a major part in steering the portfolio strategy: recently over 50 percent was invested in Europe, perhaps 25 percent was in U.S. equities, and less than 10 percent was at risk in Japan and the Pacific Rim. Hayes's bottom-up stock-picking talent consistently carries the ball over the goal line. For example, during the late 1997 Asian crisis she grabbed the opportunity to buy Microsoft, Cisco, and Worldcom before the recovery in technologies.

Hayes has been working her magic with extreme success, outperforming her global peer-group benchmark with 3-year returns in the range of 25 percent, and doing it with an expense ratio under 1.00 percent and turnover that's now under 80 percent. If you had put in $10,000 at inception in 1991, it would have grown to about $35,000 within 6 years. A solid winner.

For more information call 1-800-525-8983

T. ROWE PRICE EUROPEAN STOCK

OK, so most asset allocation models recommend diversifying as much as 25 percent of your portfolio internationally. However, blindly following this theory into emerging- and developing-nation funds makes no sense and may even produce disastrous results for a portfolio. Here's our recommendation: If you insist on investing internationally, stick to the developed-nations funds when allocating your assets. And in recent years the strongest international markets have been in Europe, with a total population of 290 million in eleven nations, a new common currency, and a vital new collective spirit that's now focusing more on American-style capitalism, including bottom-line profitability, increased shareholder values, long-term savings, corporate restructuring, and intense global competition.

Comanager James Seddon has been with the T. Rowe Price European Stock Fund since it opened up shop in London in 1990, outperforming its peer group by investing in large-cap companies with strong earnings growth. The fund is a no-load vehicle with over $1.3 billion under management, and it's growing rapidly. Its 3-year returns of around 20 percent surpass those of most of its peers, with a $10,000 investment at inception growing to almost $30,000 in the first 8 years. Beta is only 0.50 to the S&P 500. With expenses about 1.00 percent and turnover under 20 percent, this is a solid international investment in developed countries.

For more information call 1-800-638-5660

TWEEDY, BROWNE GLOBAL VALUE

Tweedy, Browne Global Value is a no-load equity fund with almost $2.5 billion in assets, a very low 20 percent turnover, and volatility only two-thirds of that of the S&P 500. Since inception in 1993 the fund has had solid returns of 15 percent, with a $10,000 investment growing to slightly over $20,000 in the first 4 years. Such performance puts it in the top 5 percent of its peer group. Global Value is managed by the same group overseeing Tweedy, Browne's $1 billion-plus American Value equity fund—Christopher Browne, William Browne, and John Spears—and this team has created a couple of winning funds.

The Tweedy, Browne Global Value team is looking for stocks in established companies trading at or near 50 percent of their inherent value. This investment strategy typically results in holding periods of 3 to 4 years and a turnover rate under 20 percent. Fortunately, during the Asian crisis they had less than 5 percent of their assets invested in the Pacific Rim. Almost 45 percent of the fund is in the developed nations of Europe, 20 percent in North America, and about 15 percent in Japan. Tweedy, Browne's managers also hedge against the risk of currency fluctuations (unlike most of their competition), adding another dimension to their conservative, highly disciplined, value-oriented approach to investing, both domestically and internationally.

For more information call 1-800-432-4789

SCUDDER GLOBAL FUND

Scudder has a broad selection of ten no-load funds investing throughout the world. William Holzer has been the lead manager of Scudder Global since its inception in 1986. He recently added two comanagers to help with this portfolio as it expands to more than $1.5 billion in assets. Holzer is a classic top-down strategist searching for global megatrends, then fitting large-cap picks with strong earnings growth into his portfolio's asset allocations. Holzer was one of the early birds in appreciating the vast opportunities inherent in the economic restructuring of Europe.

Scudder Global has a broad mandate allowing the managers to switch from 100 percent foreign to 100 percent domestic investments. In fact, Global recently had about 50 percent of its assets in European and 25 percent in U.S. stocks, with only 10 percent in Japan and the Pacific Rim. Long-term returns are strong compared with its peer group, and recent returns have been around 15 percent, closely tracking the Morgan Stanley international index. A $10,000 investment a decade ago would be valued at more than $40,000 today.

As an alternative, two other Scudder foreign-equity funds are also worth a close look: the $2.5 billion Scudder International Fund, founded in 1957, and the $1 billion Scudder Greater Europe Growth Fund, founded in 1994.

For more information call 1-800-225-2470

USAA INTERNATIONAL

The USAA International Fund, begun in 1988, is one of thirty-five in the USAA family of funds. Lead manager David Peebles has been at the helm since inception and steers a rather conservative path with this fund, whose assets are about $500 million. His portfolio is well diversified with over 150 stocks, much larger than those of most of the fund's peers. He restricts investments in any one emerging market to less than 3 percent of assets, although the total of 20 percent invested in emerging markets as a whole places the fund high among its peer group.

This fund is another solid international fund with a broad mandate: USAA International can invest 80 percent or more of its investments anywhere in the world. Yet its recent success lies in a strategic decision to shift more of its assets—recently over 70 percent—into Europe, with less than 10 percent in Japan and a small percentage in the emerging nations of the Pacific Rim.

Peebles's strategy has paid off quite well: The fund's performance has been consistently near the top of its peer group in the past 5-year period and about 10 percent recently. As a result, a $10,000 investment made at inception would have been worth about $25,000 a decade later. Moreover, Peebles does the job by holding expenses under 1.10 percent and keeping turnover under 50 percent. USAA International is an excellent choice.

For more information call 1-800-382-8722

Sector Funds

SECTOR FUNDS INVEST IN single industries, such as technology, finance, retailing, or health care. The biggest problem with sector funds is the inability of most investors and professionals to time market twists, turns, and cycles. One very successful market timer once told me that his superpowered computer system was amazingly accurate timing the daily cycles in gold futures, Swiss Francs, soybeans, and the S&P 500. But he was quick to add, "I don't have a clue what's going to happen a week from now."

Back in early 1994, my financial newsletter, the *Future News Index,* monitored about fifty market timers. Most of them were predicting a market drop of 20 percent or more in early 1995. Some of these SuperBears even forecast a total market collapse, from a Dow of 4,000 points into the 1,100 to 1,500 range. Simultaneously, these same bearish market timers were also expecting gold to jump from the $390 per ounce range to $500 and higher. Many of them sold, got out of the market, went into cash—and looked foolish several months later as the market started its bullish ride up from 4,000, while gold lost its luster, dropping into the $300 range.

REALITY CHECK: SECTOR FUNDS ARE MORE VOLATILE AND RISKY

THE FACT IS, SECTOR funds are exceptionally volatile: They will drop more in a correction or bear market, just as some may outperform in a bull market. Consider *Mutual Funds* magazine's characterization of the technology sector as an example:

> Looking for Mt.-Everest-like returns? Willing to accept death-defying downward spirals? . . . Then take a look at tech-

nology funds. They're hot again. If tech-fund shareholders have learned anything the last few years, it's that the wild rides will be followed by harrowing descents. [But] with all their volatility, many technology funds have proven to be worth the gut-wrenching ride over the long run. Of the 13 tech funds that have been around for at least 10 years, 8 have trounced the S&P 500's 289 percent cumulative returns.

Are you savvy enough to withstand the cyclical rides? If not, stick with the more steady blue chips, hybrids, and index funds.

WARNING: PLAN YOUR ASSET ALLOCATIONS FIRST

SECTOR FUNDS ARE NOT for everyone. If you'll need money for a down payment on a new home in the next few years, or even if you're saving for your children's college education in 5 to 7 years, you probably won't have many—or any—sector funds in your portfolio.

Why? It's quite simple: If you're serious about financial planning for your future—and your future's got a short-term horizon—your asset allocations will be more heavily weighted toward cash, bond funds, and blue-chip growth funds, with perhaps no more than 20 to 25 percent of your assets in some mixture of the higher-risk small-cap, global, and sector funds.

So, even if you have a 10-year or longer time horizon before you need to pull money out, it's unlikely you'll have more than 10 percent of your total portfolio in sector funds anyway. An experienced investor, familiar with a particular industry, might go higher, but if you expect to need your money sooner than 10 years—and you have a low tolerance for risk—you may want to avoid them altogether. Their volatility may result in sleepless nights.

MARKET TIMERS ACTING
LIKE BLUE-CHIP GROWTH FUNDS

ON THE OTHER HAND, if you are investing for the long run, here are the top Sector SuperStars: the "best of the best" sector funds, a group of funds that think they're solid blue-chip growth funds:

TOP-TEN SUPERSTAR SECTOR FUNDS

1 Fidelity Select Brokerage & Investment Management
2 Fidelity Select Financial Services
3 Fidelity Select Home Finance
4 Fidelity Select Regional Banks
5 Fidelity Select Healthcare
6 Fidelity Select Electronics
7 Invesco Strategic Financial
8 Invesco Strategic Health Sciences
9 Vanguard Specialized Healthcare
10 Cohen & Steers Realty

FIDELITY'S SECTOR FUND SUPERSTARS

The Olympics, the World Series, the Indy 500, the Super Bowl—like these, Fidelity has a "dream team" of sector funds. These guys need no introduction. Like Michael Jordan, Fidelity's Select Funds are in a class by themselves: Eleven of their thirty-eight sector funds appeared among our top-twenty Sector SuperStars. True, sector funds are more volatile. They certainly are more cyclical—rising and falling, in and out of favor—and therefore could quickly be replaced by some new favorite industrial sectors in a few years. They are naturally less diversified, tending to underperform benchmarks like the S&P 500 in a correction.

Despite this, for the sophisticated investor the high payoff is well worth the risk. For example, five funds in our top ten recently enjoyed 3-year average annual returns over 30 percent, besting the S&P 500 benchmark. If you're a very savvy investor—especially someone who has a working familiarity with the industry represented by a sector fund—these funds might even replace some of your growth funds.

Sector fund volatility is due to the fact that they are nondiversified, focusing narrowly on very specific industrial categories. Being volatile, cyclical, less diversified, and less predictable, sector funds are clearly best viewed as a tool intended primarily for professional market timers and sophisticated investors. In recent years, however, the financial sector has been acting more like growth funds, inviting a flood of new money chasing the obvious opportunities.

To be sure, there is a downside to the sector play at Fidelity: You pay a 3 percent load up front to get into the game; average expenses of 1.50 percent are higher than those of most stock funds; turnover of 100 to 150 percent may have an impact on your taxes; and although the SuperStars listed below are outperforming the S&P 500, Fidelity's sector funds as a whole do underperform many blue-chip stock funds.

Nevertheless, the reality is that about twenty-five of Fidelity's thirty-five sector funds are average or better within their specific categories. So if you're a street-smart, risk-tolerant, active investor, jump in and play the game. If you limit your investments in sector funds, the rewards can be quite generous and the game quite exciting.

FIDELITY SELECT BROKERAGE
& INVESTMENT MANAGEMENT
FIDELITY SELECT FINANCIAL SERVICES
FIDELITY SELECT HOME FINANCE
FIDELITY SELECT REGIONAL BANKS

Four of Fidelity's financial services sector funds are in the top-ten Sector SuperStars, a sign of the broader macroeconomic forces at work. The extraordinary growth of technology, especially the Internet, parallels the unprecedented growth in financial services, which was propelled by the collective macroeconomic forces of the late 1990s bull market, higher disposable income, on-line discount brokerage, low interest rates and inflation, increased global interest in equities, and the emergence of the new do-it-yourself investor.

In this context, it's easy to see why the financial services sector has become so popular in recent years. In fact, long-term success in financial services may be a no-brainer: The funds are riding on the momentum of unprecedented economic prosperity fueled by technological advances.

In the past five years average returns have been matching those of the S&P 500. There are a few drawbacks with Fidelity's thirty-eight Select funds: They aren't cheap; all have a 3 percent front-end load (they're the only load funds among the one hundred SuperStars); and their operating expenses tend to be higher than those of most stock funds. The average expense for these four funds is over 1.50 percent, with the highest being Select Brokerage.

However, with recent 3-year returns hovering around 30 percent annually, "Who cares?" is a typical reaction of savvy investors making sector plays. If you were lucky enough to see this sector's explosion coming, $10,000 invested in this fearsome foursome would have grown into the $70,000 range in the past decade.

Fidelity Select Brokerage & Investment Management has been around since 1985, with manager Peter Fruzzetti taking charge in 1997 after several years as an analyst. He has about 50 percent of his roughly $700 million invested in the Wall Street establishment, betting on brand names like Morgan Stanley, Merrill Lynch, Bear Sterns, Salomon Smith Barney, and PaineWebber and riding their coattails quite successfully. Long-term returns have also been solid: over 20 percent for the past decade.

Fidelity Select Financial Services is also managed by an experienced, new manager, Robert Ewing. He took over in 1996, although he has been an analyst with Fidelity since 1990. This fund opened its doors in 1981 and manages several hundred million dollars in assets. Over half the holdings are concentrated in ten institutions, like Citigroup, American Express, BancOne, Barnett, and First Chicago. Mergers have boosted performance. Short- and long-term returns are equally impressive, with the latter averaging over 20 percent for the past decade.

Fidelity Select Home Finance has also been around since 1985, with manager Bill Rubin in the driver's seat since 1994. At least 80 percent of the fund's roughly $1.1 billion in assets is invested in real estate finance institutions, solid names like Ahmanson, Dime, Washington Mutual, Chase, and Fannie Mae. With average returns near 25 percent for the past decade (although downdrafts in interest rates or the real estate industry could affect these), this is a solid fund for the long term.

Fidelity Select Regional Banks is another strong long-term performer that's been around since 1986. Christine Schaulat took the helm in early 1998 and manages over $1 billion in assets. Over 50 percent of the portfolio is in the top-ten holdings. The term "regional" is a misnomer, as the fund's investment style has shifted more toward money-center banks, with holdings in BankAmerica, First Chicago, Wells Fargo, NationsBank, and Citigroup.

A $10,000 investment here a decade ago would be worth over $100,000 today.

For more information call 1-800-544-8888

FIDELITY SELECT HEALTHCARE

Health care is another megatrend driving our economy. Aging boomers are living longer and need more care. New drugs appear regularly. Medical costs are going through the roof. Managed care has transformed the focus of the medical field from caring for people to managing the bottom line. Fidelity has been on the leading edge of this wave since starting this fund in 1981; it now has over $2 billion in assets. The manager, Beso Sikharulidze, took over the fund in 1997 after a stint as an analyst for several years. So far he's scoring high marks with recent returns close to 35 percent. Longer-term returns are equally impressive: For the past decade the fund has had average annual returns averaging about 25 percent. A $10,000 investment 10 years ago would be worth about $100,000 today.

The fund's objective is capital appreciation. Sikharulidze achieves his goal by sticking with the brand names in drugs, medical supplies, biotechnology, HMOs, and other health care delivery systems—names such as Merck, Pfizer, Eli Lilly, Bristol-Myers Squibb, and Warner-Lambert. At any one time, over 50 percent of the portfolio may be invested in just ten of these industry leaders. If the health care sector has a special interest for you, here is an excellent investment choice.

For more information call 1-800-544-8888

FIDELITY SELECT ELECTRONICS

Technology may be the single most important force driving our economy and our world forward into the new millennium. Fidelity entered this sector with several funds focusing on computers, software, telecommunications, and electronics (any one of which, as of this writing, could easily replace any one of Fidelity's four financial sector funds, based solely on short-term returns).

This electronics sector fund opened its doors in 1985 and has enjoyed long-term returns averaging over 25 percent for the past 10 years. Returns here may be a reflection more of underlying macroeconomic trends than of stock-picking magic. A $10,000 investment here 10 years ago would be worth $80,000 today, although returns have recently been relatively level.

Paul Kaplan took over as manager in 1996 and has been one of the more active managers on the Fidelity sector team. His electronics sector portfolio is concentrated, with more than 50 percent of its assets in ten stocks within this extremely volatile sector. Moreover, Kaplan is practically a day-trader, with turnover exceeding 400 percent annually—paralleling the rapid flow of new generations of technology. Don't even bother to ask about holdings. By the time you get any information about the fund's portfolio, Kaplan will already have a whole new one. But if you're savvy about the electronics sector of the economy, this is as good as it gets.

For more information call 1-800-544-8888

INVESCO STRATEGIC FINANCIAL

Should you invest in a sector fund? Many asset-allocation experts say yes. Invesco, however, encourages investors to limit sector funds to somewhere between 5 and 20 percent of their portfolios, depending on their goals. Invesco also recommends allocating your money among two or more sectors. And plan to invest in them for at least 3 years; don't use them for fast-paced trading.

Invesco Strategic Financial Services was riding the crest in this sector throughout the 1990s when we interviewed manager Jeff Morris. A SuperStar Fund with about $1.5 billion in assets and exceptional 10-year annualized returns in the 25 percent range, this fund deserves a very close second look, especially since it has the added advantage of being a no-load fund. Its primary statistics are reasonable: Beta is around 1.00, expenses are about 1.00 percent, and turnover is comfortably around 100 percent. The fund is one of eleven sector funds and a total of thirty-five funds in the Invesco family. This one has performed so well that a $10,000 investment a decade ago would be worth about $100,000 today. It's an excellent choice for an investor who wants to put money into the financial services sector.

For more information call 1-800-525-8085

INVESCO STRATEGIC HEALTH SCIENCES

Here's another first-class offering in the health care sector, an industry likely to remain hot well into the foreseeable future. Invesco got in on the ground floor back in 1985, and manager John Schroer took the helm of this $1.3 billion fund in 1994. Ten-year average returns are close to 25 percent, beating the S&P 500 and making it possible for a $10,000 initial investment to grow to about $95,000 today. Expenses are just a shade over 1.00 percent, with beta under 0.90.

Schroer has steered the fund into relatively safe waters with large-cap brand names. The portfolio is heavily concentrated in the drug industry, with over 50 percent in big-ticket names like SmithKline Beecham, Warner-Lambert, Merck, Pfizer, Schering-Plough, Bristol-Myers Squibb, and McKesson. Although close to 150 percent, turnover is reasonable. Invesco is making some excellent plays in the health care field, so maybe you should too. Discover how to succeed in health care without really trying, by riding on their coattails.

For more information call 1-800-525-8085

VANGUARD SPECIALIZED HEALTHCARE

You're probably wondering how a penny-pinching Vanguard fund wound up, like the Trojan horse, competing in the midst of Fidelity's hot hand of thirty-eight sector funds. Was it just a fluke? Or was it simply because the health care–HMO–pharmaceuticals arena has been so hot in the 1990s? After all, three health care sector funds wound up among the top-ten SuperStars here. If the health care industry is just a cyclical play, then you'd better monitor this sector (and this fund) more closely than others.

Vanguard Specialized Healthcare has been a consistently high performer for over a decade, which may explain why it was the single most highly recommended sector fund among the best-funds lists we tracked last year. The portfolio is now well over $7 billion.

Lead manager Ed Owens has been running the show since the fund's inception in 1984, and he typically beats the S&P 500, with solid picks and a scant 10 percent turnover. A $10,000 investment a decade ago would now be worth about $100,000. How does Owens dampen the usual health care sector volatility and create a measure of safety compared with his peers? It's easy. He keeps his cool, diversifying within the health care sector instead of chasing the hottest subsectors. Fortunately, picks like Bristol-Myers Squibb, Pfizer, Upjohn, and Warner-Lambert have done extremely well in recent years. And so has Owens. Longer-term returns in the 30 percent range put his fund into the top 5 percent of his peer group.

For more information call 1-800-662-7444

COHEN & STEERS REALTY

Historically, real estate prices move in long-term cycles—some researchers say in 18.2-year cycles. This sector has been recovering since 1992, driven by the bull market. A couple of years ago real estate was so hot that *Mutual Funds* magazine hailed it as the "top market sector." As a result, investors poured money into funds like Cohen &

Steers Realty (CSR), the biggest and most popular, which has grown rapidly to $2 billion.

CSR is a top-performing no-load fund with solid stats: Turnover is only 40 percent; expenses are just a hair over 1 percent; beta is under 0.40. If you'd invested $10,000 at inception in 1991 it would be worth about $25,000 today.

CSR is a good example of the cyclical nature of sector funds. Recent downturns in interest rates have affected their short-term returns and prompted some investors to jump ship. Critics argue that CSR has grown too fast, that they're too big. Although CSR is diversified across more than 200 investments, these assets are relatively small, illiquid, and difficult to unload in a major correction. CSR is not alone. Experts also criticize other giant real estate funds—like Fidelity Real Estate Investment ($2 billion) and Vanguard Specialty REIT Index ($1 billion)— for the same reason.

As with all sector funds, real estate is best left to very sophisticated investors. But if you're one of them, Cohen & Steers Reality is one of the best of the best.

For more information call 1-800-437-9912

SECTOR FUNDS ARE "the riskiest part of the domestic fund universe," warns *Mutual Funds* magazine. "But if you're after high returns, it's hard to beat those swinging sectors." And swing they do—wild and fast. As we sign off, the financial services sector is falling out of favor (it will come back), while tech funds are rocketing to ever-higher returns (they won't stay there forever). Remember, sector funds aren't for the faint of heart. Pick one or two with solid long-term track records in sectors you understand and forget short-term market timing.

America's Hybrid-Fund SuperStars

HYBRID FUNDS BLEND stocks and bonds in a single fund. Think of a hybrid fund as a one-fund mini-portfolio. Despite the differences, these funds are all one-stop, keep-it-simple solutions. Balanced funds, asset-allocation funds, and funds-of-funds attempt to build a complete portfolio for you in a single fund. They blend stocks and bonds to approximate general risk profiles, time horizons, and the need for income and capital appreciation. They are usually offered in sets of three funds, ranging from conservative to moderate to aggressive. Convertible-bond funds are also included here because they mix stocks and bonds. However, given the availability of other high-quality alternatives, they may be less appropriate for the average portfolio.

As good as these hybrid funds are, they just don't excite much *passion* in investors because they are, well, boring—and purposely so. They're designed for the following types of investors:

◆ Busy investors lacking the time, motivation, or skills to manage their assets, such as high-net-worth executives, wealthy retirees, or anyone receiving a windfall.

◆ Investors with a very low tolerance for risk.

◆ Savvy investors living real lives beyond the markets, beyond money, beyond even the material world.

Explore these hybrid categories and see what you think.

BALANCED FUNDS

UNCERTAIN ABOUT HOW to get the right mix of stocks and bonds for your portfolio? Consider this: Balanced funds are like protective parents—they let you off the hook to run and play elsewhere. They think they know exactly how much you need to allocate to each category. These guys usually keep a fixed percentage of their portfolios in stocks and in bonds: say 60 percent stocks, 40 percent bonds, or vice versa.

Since stocks and bonds are supposed to move in different cycles, their ups and downs will offset each other. Because they're so heavily loaded with bonds, balanced funds normally won't take advantage of a bullish run in the stock market. They are, however, well suited for retirees enjoying their Frosted Flakes, and for anyone else with a short-term horizon and a strong need for capital preservation.

ASSET-ALLOCATION FUNDS

THESE GUYS REALLY take all the fun out of investing. Like those awful "Got milk?" commercials, asset-allocation funds are like eating raw shredded wheat, without milk and sugar. Yuck! You feel as if you have nothing to do as an investor. Asset-allocation funds are like balanced funds, except that the managers get to have all the fun.

Unlike a balanced fund, which is locked into fixed portions of stocks and bonds, asset-allocation funds allow managers to play the market-timing game with your money. They believe they can beat the market by shifting money back and forth between stocks and bonds to take advantage of broader economic and market swings. Sometimes they do, sometimes they don't.

CONVERTIBLE-BOND FUNDS

HERE'S ANOTHER BID to split your risk between growth stocks (asset appreciation) and bonds (income and capital preservation) while getting some of the benefits of both. These funds will settle your stomach, because convertible securities tend to go up like stocks, while their inherent value as bonds cushions the downside. Meanwhile, you sit back and reap the benefits.

FUNDS-OF-FUNDS

THIS SMALL GROUP of funds invests only in other funds. Wow, you say, isn't that unimaginative? Yes. Typically you'll also find them offered in sets of three, to fit broad classes of investor needs from conservative to moderate to aggressive growth. Unfortunately, with these funds the investor is totally isolated from all the excitement and recreational value of investing. You'll never feel the real passion of Frosted Flakes investing.

THE BOTTOM LINE ON HYBRID FUNDS: A NEW PERSPECTIVE ON HAVING FUN!

I'VE MADE A DRAMATIC point here about how all these hybrid funds are boring. They are without any redeeming recreational value for our inner soul—if you love the excitement of the market. The creative, fun-loving little kid within each of us just doesn't think hybrids are very cool! But isn't that what most of us should really be looking for? Long-term investing is *supposed* to be boring! Let it be dull as dry shredded wheat. In fact, stop thinking there should be any "passion" in investing. Look elsewhere for your fun. Remember: Plan your asset allocations first, and forget market timing.

Below are our top-ten Hybrid SuperStars. Their 3-year annualized returns are included, as are their inception dates. While all of them have proven track records of at least 3 years or more, Dodge & Cox Balanced and Vanguard Wellington have both been around for about 70 years, a testament to American conservatism.

TOP-TEN HYBRID SUPERSTAR FUNDS

1 Dodge & Cox Balanced
2 Fidelity Puritan
3 Founders Balanced
4 Gabelli Westwood Balanced Retail
5 Heartland Value Plus
6 Invesco Total Return
7 Janus Balanced
8 UAM-FPA Crescent
9 Vanguard Asset Allocation
10 Vanguard Wellington

DODGE & COX BALANCED

If the Dodge & Cox Balanced Fund were a Hollywood film director, the Academy of Motion Picture Arts and Sciences would have to give it a special Oscar for lifetime achievement. It is the top ranked SuperStar Hybrid Fund and it's easy to see why. Dodge & Cox Balanced has been around since 1931. Born of the Great Depression, this fund has steered a steady course through war and peace, rock and rap, bulls and bears.

It operates on a team-management approach, with the average manager's tenure over 15 years. In an interview with John Gunn, the lead manager, we discovered why Dodge & Cox Balanced truly deserves an Oscar, and why the fund just might help make your own portfolio a winner too. After all, a $10,000 investment made 10 years ago would now be worth about $40,000, and you'd have been getting a lot of sleep.

Today they're managing over $5 billion, with roughly 50 percent in stocks, 40 percent in bonds, and the rest in cash, an asset allocation fairly typical for hybrid funds in recent years. It's a no-load fund with a low 0.60 percent expense ratio. Volatility and risk are low as well, with beta at 0.60 and turnover around 20 percent, creating a highly tax-efficient fund. Their annualized returns are about 15 percent for the past 3 years and 10 years. This fund looks like a box-office hit and Oscar contender.

For more information call 1-800-621-3979

FIDELITY PURITAN

Here's another reliable old salt. Puritan is a true-blue baby boomer, born in the postwar days of 1947—an unofficial member of AARP! This $25 billion-plus balanced fund attempts to maximize income while ensuring the preservation of investor capital. And you can't knock the results. To be sure, total returns are below those of the S&P 500. But so are those of 90 percent of all stock funds. Puritan, however, has achieved consistent average annual returns of around 15 percent for over 20 years, and it has been close to 20 percent for the past 3 years. Longevity does count. A $10,000 investment a decade ago would now be worth about $45,000.

Manager Bettina Doulton took charge in 1996 after a few years as an analyst with Fidelity. The fund's asset allocations look like this: Stocks are 60 percent, fixed income investments are 30 percent, and the rest are in high-yield bonds and cash. One big plus with Puritan is its low expense ratio: less than 0.70 percent. That's about half the category average, which is a major factor in keeping any fund consistently in the top echelons of its peer group.

For more information call 1-800-544-8888

FOUNDERS BALANCED

The best defense is a good offense. That's the kind of solid game plan manager Brian Kelly plays. Kelly took control of Founders Balanced in 1996 after a few years as a portfolio manager with Invesco. His conservative game plan favors solid, large-cap brand names like Allstate, Pfizer, SmithKline Beecham, Glaxo Wellcome, and Colgate-Palmolive. But with the fund's aggressively high turnover, averaging more than 200 percent, you can expect that these blue chips will soon be replaced with equally strong names.

This $1.2 billion fund has built a very respectable track record since it opened its doors in 1963. Long-term total returns have been around 15 percent for the past decade, with a $10,000 investment growing to about $40,000 on expenses of about 1.00 percent. Kelly is turning in a solid performance in line with long-term returns. The 30 percent bond allocation of his portfolio is grounded in intermediate U.S. Treasuries. Stocks—about 50 percent of the mix—are fundamentally strong, liquid companies with solid fundamentals and steady earnings growth.

For more information call 1-800-525-2440

GABELLI WESTWOOD BALANCED RETAIL

Susan Byrne had an outstanding track record as a money manager. In 1987, several years after first going into business, she started the large-cap Westwood Equity Retail Fund, and in 1991 she opened the doors to Westwood Balanced Retail, a hybrid. Assets are about $150 million, and given recent press exposure and the merger with Gabelli, new money is likely to lead to rapid expansion in the near future. Byrne fits Gabelli's style to a tee, as both have a strong value orientation. That approach is also at the core of her investment strategy.

Like the Equity Retail Fund, Gabelli Westwood Balanced Retail Fund is also a winner. Both use the same stock-picking strategy. The stock/bond split is about 60/40. Volatility and risk are low, with beta about half that of the S&P 500. And returns were over 15 percent for the recent 3-year period, with a $10,000 investment growing to more than $25,000 in the first 5 years. Byrne succeeds by picking companies that are cheap, with fundamentals that are much stronger than current market perceptions and in which some change agents are emerging. Byrne's formula has led to personal success; it is also paying off handsomely for the fund's shareholders. Here is a solid fund with relatively low risk and high returns over the long haul.

For more information call 1-800-937-8966

HEARTLAND VALUE PLUS

Although Heartland Value Plus is a relative newcomer among hybrid funds, the lead manager, William Nasgovitz, is a seasoned veteran. In 1984 Nasgovitz started the original Heartland Value Fund, an equity fund investing in microcaps under $300,000. As success brought in new money and the bull market added lots of competition for microcaps, Nasgovitz decided to close the fund to new investors rather than compromise his strategy. He opened Heartland Value Plus in 1993, just prior to closing Heartland Value.

The fund's asset allocations are two-thirds in microcap companies with market capitalizations around $250 million and the rest in cash and debt, including some junk bonds—definitely a contrarian strategy. This is clearly not your typical hybrid fund. Turnover is around 75 percent; beta is about half the S&P 500's. Assets are approximately $200 million and growing. Heartland Value Plus manages to perform well in a rising market, but the heavy emphasis on microcaps may well prove risky in a down market. That was apparent with Nasgovitz's other fund, Heartland Value, back in 1990, when it lost over 15 percent.

Still, Heartland Value Plus had average annual returns close to 30 percent in 1996 and 1997. Despite a flat first year, a $10,000 investment would have grown to about $20,000 in the initial 4 years of operation. In short, "when it's good, it's really good, and when it's bad. . . ." The real lesson here is that you shouldn't pay too much attention to what the prospectus or the rating agencies cite as the fund's objective. This one smells and acts more like a higher-risk small-cap fund than a relatively conservative hybrid—a very good one, but nevertheless a small-cap stock fund. This lesson is well worth learning before you invest.

For more information call 1-800-432-7856

INVESCO TOTAL RETURN

Here's a rock-solid asset-allocation hybrid fund that's weathered the bears and ridden the bull since 1987, to the tune of 15 percent total returns over the long term, over 25 percent in 1997. Net result: A $10,000 investment 10 years ago would equal about $40,000 now. Comanager Edward Mitchell has been piloting this $2.8 billion tanker on a steady course since 1987, with David Griffin joining him on the bridge in 1993.

Invesco Total Return Fund fits a classic textbook model for a hybrid fund. The Mitchell/Griffin strategy is relatively conservative: Stocks are solidly anchored in 60 to 65 percent undervalued, brand-name, blue-chip large-caps with strong earnings. Income is generated from cash plus an allocation of 25 to 30 percent in a bond portfolio of intermediate U.S. Treasuries and investment-grade corporates.

There's confidence to spare with these managers: They so totally believe in the securities they pick that turnover has been less than 10 percent in recent years, giving investors a highly tax-efficient investment. Moreover, volatility (beta) is about two-thirds the rate of the S&P 500, and at less than 1.00 percent, expenses bolster the bottom line, making Invesco Total Return a top performer among its peers and an excellent choice in virtually any conservative portfolio.

For more information call 1-800-525-8085

JANUS BALANCED

The prospectus says that Janus Balanced Fund allocates assets between stocks and bonds, normally in a range between 40 and 60 percent. On the surface, it appears to fit the bland middle-of-the-road profile of a hybrid. However, like many other funds in Janus's no-load family, the Balanced Fund leans toward growth investing, setting it apart from the competition. In fact, at one point recently manager Blaine Rollins built up a rather large and aggressive 20 percent position in convertible bonds. In equities, he's followed the lead of the $20 billion-plus aggressive flagship Janus Fund (Janus Balanced is a baby in the family, with under $1 billion), picking up some tech stocks that stumbled, small-caps, and foreign stocks, after taking profits on financial services holdings.

Rollins has been on the Janus team since 1990, a couple of years before the inception of Janus Balanced. In 1996 he became its manager, and he's a fairly active one at that: Turnover is frequently 150 percent or more, with expenses about 1.10 percent. Volatility and beta are about half the S&P 500 benchmark. Total returns are sizzling for a hybrid: They average over 20 percent for the recent 3-year period, over 15 percent for 5 years. That performance would have turned a $10,000 investment into approximately $25,000 in just 5 years. Now that Rollins's aggressive style has been tested in a real correction, it's probably a solid play in any market.

For more information call 1-800-525-8983

UAM-FPA CRESCENT

This fund's name sounds like the code word for a spy in a James Bond film. And its investment strategy is as far "out there" as its name. UAM-FPA Crescent definitely does not fit the classic textbook definition of a hybrid fund. The main objective of most hybrid funds is conservative risk diversification from mixing stocks and bonds in a single portfolio. A normal hybrid strategy demands investing in boring blue-chip stocks and investment-grade bonds. They are like Nyquil: Take it and you sleep peacefully.

Not so with manager Steven Romick's fund, which opened in 1993 and now has about half a billion dollars in assets. UAM-FPA Crescent is an anomaly like Heartland Value Plus: a pseudo-hybrid mutated by the bull market mania for maximum returns. When necessary, Romick's investment strategy blends in small-caps, micro-caps, foreign equities, convertibles, junk bonds, shorting, and large cash positions—activities more common to day-traders than conservative hybrid-fund managers. However, turnover, which used to be above 150 percent, is now below 25 percent. And the expenses reflect his approach: They are around 1.50 percent, rather high for a top-performing hybrid fund.

But Romick's mysterious alchemy is working like a charm, thank you. Returns for 1996 and 1997 were 20 percent, placing the fund high within its peer group. A $10,000 investment at inception would have put over $20,000 in your pocket in about 4 years. True, this portfolio was vulnerable in the recent correction, but in a rising market and a strong economy it's perfectly suited for today's risk-tolerant investor interested in hybrids.

For more information call 1-800-638-7983

VANGUARD ASSET ALLOCATION

Here's another slam-dunk from the penny-pinchers of the mutual fund industry. Vanguard Asset Allocation is basically controlled by a black-box quantitative model that allocates its roughly $7 billion in assets among stocks, bonds, and cash to capitalize on macro trends. The stock allocations of the fund mimic those of the Vanguard Index 500 Fund, thus capturing the steady growth of the equity markets. The bond portion duplicates the returns of the Vanguard Long-Term U.S. Treasury Portfolio. And both of those funds are solid winners on their own merits.

Lead portfolio manager William Fouse has been running the fund since its inception in 1988. The money shifts back and forth in 10 percent increments. For example, in the course of a year the model may reallocate assets back and forth from 70 percent/30 percent, to 60 percent/40 percent, to 50 percent/50 percent, up to 100 percent in any category, if necessary. Turnover varies between 50 percent and a recent 10 percent. Despite all the action, beta is under 1.00 and expenses are less than 0.50 percent.

The aggressive moves made by Fouse's black box have paid off handsomely for shareholders over the years, rewarding them with returns averaging over 16 percent annually through the ups and downs since inception, and over 20 percent in recent years. A $10,000 investment 10 years ago would be worth almost $45,000 today. It's no wonder the fund is in the rarified top 10 percent of its peer group and popular with investors and experts alike.

For more information call 1-800-662-7447

VANGUARD WELLINGTON

The very name conjures up the image of a retired British admiral, a conservative, proper old gent—and indeed it should. This fund was started way back, prior to the crash of 1929, and is still going strong with approximately $25 billion in assets. It's peppy, almost as if it's been on a steady regimen of Viagra for decades—perhaps reflecting Pfizer's position among the top 50 of its 350 holdings. Like other funds with such longevity, a stuffy fund such as this one gets less attention from young financial reporters than it does from older and wiser investors.

Wellington obviously has a strong appeal to the more conservative investor. It certainly is not as aggressive an asset-allocation fund as its sibling, the Vanguard Asset Allocation Fund. The stats reflect the difference: Beta is under 0.70 and turnover hovers around 30 percent. As expected, expenses are vintage Vanguard, around 0.30 percent.

Two comanagers split responsibilities for stocks and bonds in the fund. Stocks have been managed by Ernst von Metzsch since 1995, and the bond allocation has been run by Paul Kaplan since 1994. Allocations between the two classes vary, with stocks lately in the 60 percent range. The result is a fairly consistent performance of 15 percent for the past 15 years. In fact, a $10,000 investment back then would be worth about $40,000 today. For one of the granddaddies of all funds, this one's acting more like an energetic teenager.

For more information call 1-800-662-7447

SECTION 16

Index Funds

THERE ARE ONLY ABOUT 250 index funds, with perhaps $200 billion in total assets. This is mere pocket change compared with the $5 trillion-plus invested in all mutual funds. Yet index funds are a hot item. Some 30 new index funds are added annually—over 100 in a recent 3-year period—with investors pouring 20 to 25 percent of all new fund money into the category. What's the attraction? It's obvious. Since 80 percent of all mutual funds can't beat the indexes, investors are wising up and turning to passively managed index funds.

Fortunately, these market robots do their job incredibly well. For example, the granddaddy and still the front-runner, Vanguard's Index 500 Fund, has an annual return of about 16 percent for 15 years, beating over 80 percent of the total number of diversified equity stock funds with the same longevity, about 260.

TOP-TEN INDEX FUND SUPERSTARS

1 Vanguard Index Total Stock Market
2 Vanguard Index 500
3 Vanguard Index Growth
4 Vanguard Index Value
5 Vanguard Index Small-Cap Stock
6 Vanguard International Equity European
7 Vanguard Total Bond Market
8 Vanguard Star
9 Schwab 1000 Fund
10 T. Rowe Price Equity Index 500

FIVE REASONS TO INVEST IN INDEX FUNDS

MONEY MAGAZINE presented these compelling reasons to park your savings in index funds.

1 "Smart-bomb" accuracy. Remember those fascinating television shots during Desert Storm? Smart bombs and heat-seeking missiles with pinpoint accuracy, heading right down chimneys? Well, index funds are even more accurate, hitting their target indexes within 0.2 percent on the average.

2 Bargain-basement expenses. Equity funds pile on expenses that average more than 1.4 percent, in spite of their subpar performances. Meanwhile, the index robots match their benchmarks for half that price or less, averaging about 0.7 percent expense ratios.

And get this: the leader, Vanguard Index 500 Fund, charges a super-low ratio of only 0.19 percent. In fact, as Gus Sauter, the brains sitting behind the Vanguard Index computers, says, "The whole reason indexing works to begin with is that it's cheap."

3 Lower taxes for investors. The index funds aren't gun-slinging stock-pickers like the equity-fund hotshots. They're simply replicating a specific index. And because they're less trigger-

If you're serious about adding some index funds to your portfolio, check their Web sites or call them and get the facts. Do a little comparison shopping. Find out what makes them tick. These index funds may be just the low-stress, low-risk solution you're looking for.

VANGUARD INDEX FUNDS

VANGUARD IS THE undisputed king of index funds. Vanguard's founder John Bogle once said, "No actively managed fund has outpaced an index fund over the past 15-year period." So why not build your entire port-

happy, they trade less. So they have fewer capital-gains distributions. You wind up with more money at year-end.

4 Predictable asset allocations. OK, so you're street smart,
you have a financial plan. You have your asset allocations figured
out: your mix of stocks, bonds, cash and other assets. But unfortunately, if you give your money to some gun-slinging equity-fund
managers, they're likely to be all over the map, screwing up your
allocations, buying and selling and buying. Some managers invest
as much as 50 percent of the assets of their so-called "stock" allocation in bonds or cash. At other times, only 10 percent. The problem is you're never sure until after the fact. In contrast, index
funds stay close to their stated objectives, using weighted averages of the composition of their benchmark index, with virtually
no investment discretion. It's a predictable slam-dunk.

5 Low-stress no-brainers. With index funds you can forget
about picking the "right" top-gun manager, or the hottest sectors, or even whether you should be in blue chips or microcaps,
value or growth funds. Most of those managers can't beat the
indexes anyway. Just deposit your money in a few funds that simply track benchmarks you know work.

folio by indexing? It sure sounds like a great idea.

In fact, the idea's catching on big time. Thanks to
today's growing interest in the "efficient market theory"—
the idea that in today's extremely diverse market, active
stock-picking does not add value—indexing is now a
strategy in wide use by individual investors. Some experts
even claim that as many as 25 percent of all investors are
using it today.

Vanguard's no-load index funds are the perfect vehicle
for individual investors who are ready for this ultimate
"keep-it-simple" method of building a successful port-

folio. Vanguard has not just one but eight of the top-ten SuperStars in the category. The reasons are quite simple: **1** Vanguard's fund shareholders—not outside stockholders—own the company, so the margin of profit accrues to the benefit of the investors in its funds. **2** There are no loads or commissions. **3** Expenses are often as low as 10 to 20 percent of those of the competition. **4** There is no expensive company research involved in tracking an index. **5** Turnover is low, with maximum after-tax benefits.

George U. "Gus" Sauter has been managing equity-index funds for Vanguard since the bottom of the market in October 1987. He's the undisputed crown prince of indexing. My first image of him was a full-page picture in a *Mutual Funds* magazine article with the caption "Mr. Index, Gus Sauter, the guru behind Vanguard Index 500, is finally getting some respect." He posed smiling, seated in front of several personal computers. The article opened with an amusing anecdote: "How many people does it take to run an index fund? Answer: A thousand, one to turn on the computer and 999 to take all of the phone calls from eager investors."

When I met Gus later, I mentioned the picture and jokingly asked him if he was able to manage his billions on a single 486 computer. He quickly replied that they had actually started with a much slower 286 and that it did the job quite well, thank you. No wonder Vanguard's expenses are rock bottom. Today Gus Sauter is the lead manager responsible for about seven equity-index funds with over $100 billion in assets.

Here's a look at the eight Vanguard index funds that dominate this top-ten SuperStar category. There's a little something for everybody's portfolio. Find out why so many savvy investors today are building their portfolios by diversifying their asset allocations across Vanguard's index funds and simply riding the market to a winning portfolio.

VANGUARD INDEX TOTAL STOCK MARKET

Here's how Sauter described their Total Stock Market index fund: "[It] really is the entire U.S. stock market. It's attempting to mirror the performance of the entire U.S. stock market as measured by the Wilshire 5000. That index contains, oddly, about 7,500 stocks that trade on a regular basis on the NYSE, AMEX, or Nasdaq exchanges. We use a sampling technique there because of the large number of names and the illiquidity of many of them. We actually own about 2,900 of them." Sauter has been in command since inception in 1992. Average returns have been in the range of 20 percent for the first 5 years, and a $10,000 investment would have grown to the $25,000 range.

Thanks to some kickers in the one-third of its portfolio invested in small- and mid-caps, this broader market fund has even been outperforming the S&P 500, although on a longer-term basis it slightly underperforms the benchmark. Still, Sauter is supremely confident about this fund, making this recommendation: "For a domestic stock portfolio you could build the entire portfolio with one fund. The Total Stock Market index fund is great one-stop shopping. It gives you the broadest diversification you can ever have, covering the entire U.S. market."

For more information call 1-800-662-7447

VANGUARD INDEX 500

According to Sauter, "Our other index funds target areas of the overall market. We tend to think of the market along the lines of Morningstar's nine style boxes, where you break up the market into large, medium, and small; value, growth, and broadly diversified. The S&P 500 portfolio we would characterize as large-cap diversified." This fund has a track record stretching back to 1976, with Sauter at the helm since 1987.

The Vanguard Index 500 Fund duplicates the stock composition and weightings of the S&P 500. Moreover, at 5 percent, turnover is almost nonexistent. At 0.19 percent, expenses are so low that Gus can't help beating the competition, those actively managed stock funds whose expenses average 1.40 percent, or seven times as high as Vanguard's. And beat them he does on a regular basis. Returns of 20 to 25 percent virtually equal those of the S&P 500. A $10,000 investment a decade ago would now be worth about $60,000. No wonder he's attracted over $75 billion in assets. But don't worry: If they close this winning Godzilla, you can bet they'll quickly open "Son of Vanguard Index 500."

For more information call 1-800-662-7447

VANGUARD INDEX GROWTH

This one is a "large-cap growth-oriented fund, and includes the half of the S&P 500 that is growth oriented," says Sauter. Morningstar says a "growth" investment approach "looks for equity securities with high rates of revenue growth." In addition, the growth stocks on the industry standard SP/BARRA Growth Index typically trade at pricey multiples: higher than average price-to-earnings and price-to-book ratios.

However, if you're hesitant about agreeing totally with Sauter—that is, you don't want to put all your eggs in one basket—try the Vanguard Index Total Stock Market fund, as he suggests. But if you prefer to diversify your large-cap portfolio allocations yourself, between so-called growth and value stocks, this is the first half of this dynamic duo.

The Vanguard Index Growth Fund manages assets of approximately $4 billion. At approximately 25 percent, turnover is aggressively higher than that of the larger index funds, although expenses remain locked down at 0.20 percent. The fund has been beating the S&P 500 quite well for the past few years, with 3-year average returns in the range of 25 percent, another peer-group leader. If you'd invested $10,000 here at inception in late 1992, it would have been worth about $30,000 5 years later.

For more information call 1-800-662-7447

VANGUARD INDEX VALUE

Here's the other half of Vanguard's dynamic growth index duo, tracking the SP/BARRA Value Index. Morningstar says, "A value approach focuses on stocks that an investor or fund manager thinks are currently undervalued in price and will eventually have their worth recognized by the market." These stocks have low price-to-book ratios and higher yields. This index tends to be underweighted in the less capital-intensive industries, such as service industries, and overweighted in companies like utilities that are capital intensive.

Vanguard's Value Index Fund has been doing well, managing over $2 billion in assets. Remarkably well. Returns do parallel its benchmark, about 20 percent for the past 3 years, and it's slightly under the S&P 500. Still, performance is strong enough to beat a large majority of funds in its peer group. In fact, a $10,000 investment at inception in late 1992 would have been worth more than $25,000 after 5 years. Sauter has been managing both the large-cap Growth Index and the Value Index, as well as the Total Stock Market index, since 1992.

For more information call 1-800-662-7447

VANGUARD INDEX SMALL-CAP STOCK

Financial planners typically advise more aggressive investors to diversify some of their portfolios' asset allocations into small-cap stock funds, seeking a mix of anywhere from 10 percent to 40 percent depending on risk tolerance. Vanguard's Small-Cap Index fund has been around since 1960, with almost $3 billion in assets today. And like Vanguard's other index funds, it is fully invested, with minimal cash to drag down returns. Turnover and expenses are also much lower than those of the average small-cap stock fund.

Gus Sauter has also been managing this fund since the crash of 1987 and doing quite well. In recent years the fund has closely tracked or beaten its benchmark, the Russell 2000 small-stock index, with 10-year returns over 10 percent. As a result, a $10,000 investment made a decade ago would now be worth almost $40,000.

From an asset-allocation perspective, if you want to build a totally indexed portfolio with a single mutual fund family, rather than a funds supermarket, stick with Vanguard and blend in this small-cap fund to fit your asset-allocation goals.

For more information call 1-800-662-7447

VANGUARD INTERNATIONAL EQUITY EUROPEAN

Gus Sauter has been managing the Vanguard International Equity European index fund since inception in 1990. The fund is designed to duplicate the MSCI (Morgan Stanley Capital Index) Europe Index, which favors large-caps and established markets. Five-year returns have tracked the index rather closely in recent years, hovering around 20 percent and coming surprisingly close to S&P 500 returns. Moreover, a $10,000 investment at inception would have been worth about $25,000 just 7 years later. Volatility as measured by beta is about 0.60, well below that of the S&P 500. Expenses are only 0.30 percent, more than a point below those of the rather high-priced competition in this peer group.

As an actively managed alternative to this European index fund, consider the Vanguard International Growth Fund, a capital-appreciation fund managed by Richard Foulkes in London. Foulkes has been on the job since the doors opened in 1981. Assets under management are in the range of $8 billion, and expenses fluctuate under 0.60 percent. The fund tracks the broader

MSCI EAFE (Europe, Australia, Far East) index. Performance has been affected by the Asian crisis, as well as a failure to hedge against currency devaluations. However, Foulkes is actively correcting his portfolio, including a reduction of holdings in Japan.

For more information call 1-800-662-7447

VANGUARD TOTAL BOND MARKET

Bond index fund manager Ken Volpert told us that the "Total Bond Market Index Fund is managed against the Lehman Brothers Aggregate Bond index. This is our biggest bond index fund with $7 billion in assets. It has a third mortgage-backed, a third corporates, and a third governments. As an enhancement strategy we are a little heavier weighted in corporate bonds than the index that we're compared against. This 'corporate substitution strategy' overweights us in 1- to 4-year corporates and underweights 1- to 4-year Treasuries." And there are no junk bonds.

When I asked how their "corporate substitution strategy" worked, Volpert replied:

> In the short end of the corporate market, you get a lot more yield per unit of risk. It's a very safe area of the curve to take corporate credit exposure. Spreads widen because the duration is so short and the interest rate risk is so limited in the short end of the curve. So you have a lot more spread widening protection.
>
> If there's a recession or any kind of economic weakness, the short end is going to hold up much better than the long end of the corporate curve. A lot more protection. That's why we do that: The downside is very limited, and the upside is pretty enduring because that additional yield comes from the corporate market.

In 1992 Volpert joined veteran Vanguard bond strategist Ian MacKinnon in running the fund. With total returns of 7 to 8 percent, the fund consistently matches the Lehman Brothers Aggregate Bond index. A $10,000 investment made a decade ago would be worth about $25,000 these days. This bond index fund is a solid first choice of many investors and experts alike.

For more information call 1-800-662-7447

VANGUARD STAR

Why is this hybrid, balanced fund-of-funds listed here with the index funds? Think about it. Here's a fund investing in relatively fixed proportions in nine other widely diversified funds. It's virtually an index unto itself. But if you're one of the new breed of do-it-yourself investors and you feel more comfortable calling it a hybrid, you decide and switch it. Do your own analysis. We just wanted to get you thinking once again about the name game being played by the fund companies and their spin doctors.

So why is Vanguard Star so important? After I interviewed the manager of an independently run fund-of-funds, one reader challenged me: "I have a major concern about using the fund-of-funds approach: the extra layer of fees. If I pay the typical 1 percent fee to a fund-of-funds manager on top of the annual operating expenses of each fund—which can average between 1 and 2 percent—the resulting 2 percent to 3 percent annual cost can be a tremendous drag on overall performance."

That investor makes a good point: The two-tier expenses for independently managed funds-of-funds bother most investors, who are quickly learning that they can easily buy into a no-load fund-of-funds. Or they can create what amounts to their own fund-of-funds by using one of today's "no-transaction-fee" fund supermarkets, such as Schwab's Mutual Fund OneSource.

However, is an in-house fund-of-funds really any better just because it may be a no-load? So what if there's no double counting of expenses; the bottom-line question is, how well do they perform? We got our answer from one of our top-ten SuperStars, Jeff Molitor, manager of the Vanguard Star Fund, a fund-of-funds that invests in nine other Vanguard index funds and technically has zero expenses (although the expenses of the underlying funds average 0.35 percent). At $8 billion, this no-load fund is also the largest in its peer group. Turnover is only 15 percent; beta is 0.60; and long-term annualized returns are in the range of 15 percent. These are impressive stats for any conservative investor. In fact, a $10,000 investment in Vanguard Star a decade ago would be worth about $40,000 today.

I asked Molitor, "What's the difference between the two basic types of funds-of-funds, the independent and the in-house funds?" His answer was directly to the point: "Fees. Fees, it's basically that simple. If you look at the funds that are at organizations such as Vanguard, there is no fee for the overall fund itself. The only expenses reflect the expenses of the underlying portfolios. It's the same thing as if an individual investor went and put the package together themselves, but they just have the convenience, and that comes for free. The externally managed ones have a fee on top of those funds."

For more information call 1-800-662-7447

SCHWAB 1000 FUND®

The Charles Schwab family now has 32 no-load funds, plus Mutual Fund OneSource, a no-transaction-fee supermarket covering about 1000 funds. One of Schwab's most popular funds is the Schwab 1000 Fund®, an index fund with over $5.7 billion in assets. This index fund is a weighted average of the 1,000 largest companies, and it actually tracks the S&P 500 quite closely, with annual returns close to 20 percent. As portfolio manager Geri Hom put it, "They've outperformed about 80 percent of actively managed funds over the past ten years." In fact, a $10,000 investment at inception in 1991 would have been worth about $35,000 after 7 years.

Schwab's influence extends far beyond any one fund. They've been a pioneer on the cutting edge of the Wall Street cyberspace revolution since the mid-1970s. Phase one: Schwab challenged Wall Street with discount brokerage. Phase two: Schwab led the charge into pre-Internet electronic trading in the 1980s. Phase three: In the 1990s Web investing exploded with new opportunities, and Schwab was there. Phase four: Schwab is now the first of the discount brokers to offer full services on-line, still leading the cyberspace investing revolution into the new millennium.

By 2010, we estimate that 100 percent of all investors will have on-line accounts, a new critical mass controlling the world's financial markets. Schwab's team has a clear vision of the future of investing in America, and investors agree, for Schwab's market capitalization now exceeds that of Merrill Lynch. The highly successful Schwab 1000 is another specific example of how well they are serving the Main Street investor.

For more information call 1-800-435-4000

T. ROWE PRICE EQUITY INDEX 500
Do you think one index fund is just as good as another at tracking the S&P 500? Think again. The so-called "full-service" or full-commission Wall Street brokers frequently tack on loads and/or higher expenses to their basic index funds.

Talk about wasting money. Anyone who sells an index fund with a load is taking advantage of their customers' naïveté. Such tactics border on fraud. So it's no surprise that none of the SuperStar Index Funds is offered by Wall Street's establishment brokers; they're loading on too many expenses and commissions that provide no added value.

The T. Rowe Price family of no-loads is fanatical about cloning the index: attempting to duplicate exactly the weightings of all stocks. Expenses are about 0.40 percent—much lower than those of the average stock fund, but still higher than Vanguard's family-wide average index fee of 0.20 percent. Still, since opening its doors in 1990 this fund's average return has reliably moved within a point of that of the S&P 500: about 16 percent. A $10,000 investment back then would have grown to about $40,000 over the next 8 years. Stick with the no-load families, especially when it comes to index funds. They're no-brainers that put more money in your pocket.

For more information call 1-800-638-5660

Fixed-Income Bond Funds: Corporate, U.S. Government Securities, and Tax-Exempt Municipal Bond Funds

BOND FUNDS MAKE UP about 40 percent of all funds, over $2 trillion. They include all funds investing in the fixed-income securities of corporations (including investment-grade, blue-chip, and high-yield junk bonds), as well as government securities, U.S. Treasuries, and municipal bonds. Both taxable and tax-free bonds are included in this category.

But first, ask yourself if you really need bond funds in your portfolio. Possibly not, if your time horizon is greater than 10 years. Most investors with long-term time frames (people under 50, for example) are comfortable with portfolios loaded with 80 to 100 percent stock funds. They plan to capitalize on long-term appreciation and beat inflation, while riding out the shorter-term market cycles. However, as you get closer to the time for withdrawals, the potential need for bonds or bond funds increases.

"They may not fly like stocks, but they won't crash and burn either," says *SmartMoney* magazine, and "if you are willing to put in the effort, you're better off buying individual bonds instead of bond funds. You can tailor a portfolio of bonds exactly to your circumstances, meaning the bonds will mature when you need them.

And by holding the bonds to maturity, you eliminate the risk that rising interest rates will cut into your investment."

How much does your need for fixed income depend on your perceptions, rather than the reality of the market's direction? On whether you're a bull or a bear by temperament? On how much you think the market is going down or up in the next quarter or year?

On the other hand, is your portfolio's need for bonds and bond funds independent of the timing of market swings? (Yes.) Should the decision to put bonds in your portfolio be primarily a function of your asset allocations? (Yes.) And should you avoid increasing or decreasing the bond-fund slice of your portfolio's asset allocations just because the market rallies or corrects? (Yes.)

IT ALL DEPENDS ON
YOUR ASSET ALLOCATIONS

I'LL DIG MORE INTO your decision regarding a portfolio strategy in Part 3, but for now keep these three fundamentals in mind:

1 Forget the gurus' predictions. The decision regarding the amount of bonds in your portfolio should be a function of your risk tolerance and asset allocations, not market swings.

2 Diversify and spread your risk. As *Kiplinger's Personal Finance Magazine* suggests, you should allocate and pick your bond fund assets (including money-market funds) first, "to smooth out the volatility" of your portfolio, with the remaining segment of your portfolio appropriately diversified over several asset classes.

3 Stick within 5 percent of your allocations. Just like a professional money manager, you should rebalance and bring your asset allocations back into line with your originally planned portfolio strategy whenever your asset allocations deviate from the mark by more than 5 percent.

Find out what works for you, and how bonds fit into your strategy. And, assuming you are a long-term, buy-and-hold investor, make your decision independent of market swings.

THE TOP-TWENTY BOND FUND SUPERSTARS: LONG-TERM WINNERS

HERE ARE THE TOP-TWENTY bond fund SuperStars. Each fund must have a minimum 3-year track record to qualify initially. However, as it turns out, sixteen of the top twenty have a decade or more of solid performance behind them. Northeast Investors Trust is the granddaddy at almost 50 years old.

These bond fund SuperStars include funds investing in corporate blue chips and high-yield bonds as well as government tax-free bonds and Treasuries. There's something here to fit almost anyone's special circumstances.

The top-ten government bond SuperStars would also give the global-funds category a run for the money based on their recent 3-year performance.

TOP-TEN CORPORATE BOND FUNDS

1 Loomis Sayles Bond
2 Northeast Investors Trust
3 Fidelity High-Income
4 Harbor Bond
5 Strong Corporate Bond
6 Strong Advantage
7 T. Rowe Price Spectrum Income
8 Vanguard Fixed-Income Short-Term Corporate
9 Vanguard Fixed-Income High-Yield Corporate
10 Nicholas Income Fund

TOP-TEN GOVERNMENT BOND FUNDS

1 Vanguard Municipals Long-Term
2 Vanguard Municipals Intermediate-Term
3 Vanguard Municipals Short-Term
4 Vanguard Municipals High-Yield
5 T. Rowe Price Tax-Free High-Yield
6 Strong High-Yield Municipals
7 Vanguard Fixed-Income Long-Term U.S. Treasuries
8 Vanguard Fixed-Income GNMA
9 Strong Government Securities
10 American Century–Benham Target Maturity 2020

Whoever said "bonds are boring" sure wasn't looking at these top-performing bond fund SuperStars. Here you have the best of both possible worlds: relatively high returns and relative safety.

We wouldn't necessarily recommend that you create an entire portfolio of these bond funds, but it is certainly a tempting approach, especially if you're a conservative retiree living off the income of your portfolio, or any other type of investor with a short-term horizon.

CORPORATE BOND FUNDS

LOOMIS SAYLES BOND

You think bond funds are boring? Think again. The 1990s have given the investing public a case of bull-market mania. The decade encouraged investors to pull billions out of funds and go directly into the stock market, convinced they could outperform all those puny professional fund managers, most of whom rarely beat the major indexes anyway.

Warning! Before you yank every nickel out of your fund portfolio—and especially if you're a conservative investor looking for some balance, income, and protection in your portfolio—take a peek at the Loomis Sayles Bond Fund. It has about $1.5 billion managed by Daniel Fuss, who's been running the show since its inception in 1991.

Both current income and solid capital growth are here. Expenses are about 0.75 percent, with turnover around 40 percent. Fuss keeps 65 percent of your money locked into solid, investment-grade, corporate-debt securities, and the rest in higher-risk investments rated triple-B grade or below.

Talk to a manager like Fuss and you can feel his enthusiasm and passion for bonds, an oddity in a world that prefers the current racetrack thrills of equities. Paradoxically, Fuss also has a keen sense that people invest in bond funds because they truly *want* bond funds to be boring—steady with no surprises, so that you sleep peacefully every night.

Fuss is a total iconoclast: In listening to him you get the feeling he must be psychologically wired into national and world capital markets, somewhere between *Touched by an Angel* and *The Twilight Zone*. Whatever it is, his magic touch has pulled 10 percent average returns out of the bond market during the past 5 years. A $10,000 investment with Dan back at inception in 1991 would have grown to almost $25,000 7 years later. With him at the helm, you'll sleep well and still discover that bonds are far from boring.

For more information call 1-800-633-3330

NORTHEAST INVESTORS TRUST

Rule one: Bet on the jockey. One hundred money managers said their key criterion in picking a mutual fund was exactly that—the jockey, the fund manager. Here's one of the best on the track. Northeast Investors Trust opened its doors to investors in 1950. Ernest E. Monrad took the reins in 1960, and Northeast has been a perennial favorite ever since. In 1996 he returned 20 percent. Although short-term returns are flat, long-term returns average over 10 percent, remarkable for a fixed-income fund in a market in which, without hesitation, most brokers will recommend almost any bond fund returning over 5 percent.

Although Northeast's portfolio includes below-investment-grade securities, it's not out chasing overpriced junk bonds. Assets include established companies and $2 billion under management. Large holdings have included companies like MGM Grand, Time-Warner, Vons, Chubb, and Bankers Trust.

No wonder it's one of the top bond funds among our SuperStars, a reflection of today's aggressive markets. A $10,000 investment in this fund a decade ago would be worth about $30,000 today. Performance is based in large part on control of key statistics: Expenses are only 0.60, and turnover is only 0.30, quite low compared with the competition.

For more information call 1-800-225-6704

FIDELITY HIGH-INCOME

Call them high-yield, high-income, or junk bonds, they're simply bonds with credit ratings lower than investment grade. The dynamic junk-bond market is now close to half a trillion dollars strong. Staying on top of it demands constant attention, which it gets from a savvy bond fund manager like Fidelity's Thomas T. Soviero. He's backed by one of the largest, if not the strongest, teams of research analysts in the high-yield corporate-bond arena.

Their disciplined bottom-up style gives Soviero an edge in screening the flood of new issues in the highly sensitive arena of bonds rated B or below, and it allows them to concentrate on preferred sectors like broadcasting, cable, and telecommunications. Over 75 percent of their portfolio is well positioned in these higher-risk bonds and preferreds. The expense ratio is 0.80.

Fidelity's High-Income Fund has been around since 1990, with assets recently passing the $2.5 billion mark. Soviero took over the responsibility for running the fund in 1996 after several years as a bond research analyst. In recent years the fund has been outperforming the Lehman Brothers Aggregate Bond index, as well as its corporate high-yield peers, with average total returns in the 9 to 11 percent range. If you'd invested $10,000 here at inception it would have been worth about $30,000 7 years later.

For more information call 1-800-544-8888

HARBOR BOND

Manager William H. Gross has been called the "Peter Lynch of bonds." (Just in case you didn't know, Lynch is the great portfolio manager who built Fidelity Magellan Fund into a giant by outperforming the competition by wide margins every year.) Gross has been in charge of the Harbor Bond Fund since it began in 1987, working his magic to generate maximum total returns in the intermediate bond arena. With over 80 percent of the portfolio in single- to triple-A-rated securities, you know this is definitcly not a junk-bond fund. Success in recent years has expanded the fund into the half-billion-dollar range. Expenses are under 0.70 percent.

Gross's research begins with the broader economic issues: a top-down strategy searching for optimum yield-curve plays and rotating through the best sectors of the longer-term bond market. If this sounds as if the guy's a market timer—predicting interest-rate futures, switching sectors, and acting on yield plays—he is. But then, in the bond business, as unfavorable as it may be, you have to be a closet market timer or the credit markets will trample you.

The strategy works for Gross and his submanager, PIMCO. They are one of the best fixed-income bond fund management teams around today. Their performance speaks for itself: Total returns have been in the 8 to 10 percent range in recent years, regularly beating the intermediate bond index benchmark, enough so that a $10,000 investment with the Gross/PIMCO team the past decade would be worth over $25,000 today.

For more information call 1-800-422-1050

STRONG CORPORATE BOND

Founded in 1974 by Richard Strong, the Strong family of funds currently manages more than $30 billion. This team prides themselves in "getting it right," as they tell the world, offering investors a wide range of 100 percent no-load funds that can be used to fit virtually any individual needs. This fund has been around since 1985, with manager Jeffrey Koch taking over responsibilities in 1991; he was joined in 1995 by John Bender. Assets are in the neighborhood of $1 billion, with maturities of 7 to 12 years.

The fund has carved out a unique niche in the corporate-bond field. A large majority of its investments—perhaps 75 to 80 percent—are solidly in the double- or triple-B issues, distinguishing it from most other corporate-bond funds. As a result, the fund's an excellent counterpoint to other bond funds if you're creating a truly diverse bond portfolio.

Koch and Bender use a top-down investment strategy, balancing duration, yield-curve, and sector plays, combined with disciplined securities selection. As a result they regularly beat their peer group and the Lehman Brothers Corporate Bond index, generating yields in the range of 8 to 9 percent over the recent 3- to 5-year period, with normal volatility. A $10,000 investment here a decade ago would now be worth almost $25,000. In spite of above-normal expenses at 1 percent, the Strong family is living up to its motto and "getting it right" with this corporate-bond portfolio.

For more information call 1-800-368-1030

STRONG ADVANTAGE

Want a really short-term fund that's got about as much volatility as your checking account, yet is virtually guaranteed to beat your money-market fund? Seriously: The beta of the Strong Advantage Fund is a low, low 5 percent of the Lehman Brothers Aggregate Bond index. That's their goal: a very-low-volatility fund that knocks the socks off money-market performance. And, by God, they do achieve it, come hell or high water. How? Simply by selecting bonds with an average 6-month duration, including funds approaching their call dates, and a mix of asset classes for risk management. This fund is like valet parking for your spare cash!

The Strong family created this $2.5 billion-plus bond fund back in 1988. Jeffrey Koch has been senior manager since 1991, with Lyle Fitterer as backup quarterback. The level of credit risk is definitely higher than that of a money-market fund. Still, 75 percent of the fund's portfolio must be in investment-grade credits, with only 20 percent in B-rated securities. As a result, the performance of this management team has been extraordinary: Total returns are in the range of 6 to 7 percent. And despite the modest risk/return profile, a $10,000 investment in Strong Advantage a decade ago would be worth about $20,000 today. Now *that* is a winning money-market fund.

For more information call 1-800-368-1030

T. ROWE PRICE SPECTRUM INCOME

Here's another unique winner, one of T. Rowe Price's three funds-of-funds. Manager J. Peter Van Dyke has carved out an eclectic, hybrid income fund that invests in a diversified group of nine other T. Rowe Price income-driven funds. These include Short-Term, Long-Term U.S. Treasuries, International, GNMA, Emerging Markets, High-Yield, New Income, Summit Cash, and the Equity-Income Fund.

The Spectrum Income Fund has been in existence since 1990, with Van Dyke perfecting his role as captain of the ship, managing over $2.5 billion in assets. Obviously the fund's objective is current income and capital preservation. There are no fees other than those of the underlying funds, which range between 0.60 percent and 0.80 percent. Turnover is in the range of 15 percent. With 3- and 5-year average annual returns about 8 to 9 percent, the Spectrum Income Fund is an excellent choice for any portfolio's fixed-income allocations. A $10,000 investment here a decade ago would be worth over $22,000 today.

For more information call 1-800-638-5660

VANGUARD FIXED-INCOME SHORT-TERM CORPORATE

A couple of years ago *Money* magazine's guru Jason Zweig dubbed Vanguard bond fund manager Ian MacKinnon "The Man with the Golden Funds." A play on the title of a James Bond film, the moniker underscores how portfolio managers have become box-office celebrities in today's bull market. MacKinnon and costars Chris Ryon and Robert Auwaerter are armed with Vanguard's low expense ratio rather than 007's trusty Walther PPK as they outfox the competition. The guy must be doing something right. He's been headlining the marquee since the theater opened its doors in 1982. And he's selling a lot of tickets, with over $5 billion in assets under management.

Short-term corporate bonds make sense for investors who need a reasonably high level of current income with minimum risk. Capital and liquidity are their main features. So these SuperStars invest in investment-grade bonds with average maturities from 1 to 3 years, thus minimizing some of the volatility typical of interest-rate-sensitive, longer-term debt. Beta is about 0.50 of the S&P 500, and the expense ratio is under 0.30 percent. As a result, total returns in the range of 7 to 8 percent have been typical over the years, regularly beating the Lehman Brothers 1- to 3-Year Bond index benchmark and keeping MacKinnon and his team consistently in the top half of their peer group. If you'd invested $10,000 with these guys a decade ago you'd have over $22,000 today. Mission accomplished, 007.

For more information call 1-800-662-7447

VANGUARD FIXED-INCOME HIGH-YIELD CORPORATE

Here's another long-distance runner on the Vanguard track team. Manager Earl McEvoy has been running the fund, which was started back in 1978, since 1983. McEvoy is a true marathoner. He distinguishes himself from the rest of the competition by reaching for the higher-quality junk bonds, sacrificing some returns, going for safety in typical Vanguard fashion, and avoiding the riskier high-yield bonds. There are no speculative surprises here: no zero-coupon bonds, no bonds below a B rating. Turnover is typically under 50 percent, expenses are 0.28 percent, and beta is about 0.75.

McEvoy runs a good race. Performance is solid: Long-term total returns have hovered around 10 to 15 percent for the past 5 years. As you might expect, since he runs a relatively conservative race for a junk-bond manager, McEvoy's returns are slightly under the high-yield peer benchmark and those of the competition. However, he typically beats the broader Lehman Brothers Aggregate Bond index. If you had invested $10,000 here a decade ago, you would have over $27,000 today. With $5 billion in assets and growing, obviously a lot of investors are betting on McEvoy to continue winning races.

For more information call 1-800-662-7447

NICHOLAS INCOME FUND

Here's a corporate high-yield bond fund that's been around since the dawn of mutual fund history. Its date of inception is 1930. A father-son team manages this outstanding fund with $250 million in assets. Albert O. Nicholas began managing the fund in 1977, and in 1996 he turned the direct responsibilities over to his son, David O. Nicholas, who also manages their $5 billion equity stock fund. Nicholas Income positions itself conservatively in the intermediate-yield range with maturities of 7 to 8 years.

It's high-yield, yes, but not your typical junk-bond fund. The Nicholas team and the fund are basically very conservative. Safety is a key element in their strategy, perhaps reflected in their inclusion of up to 50 percent in utility company credits. Risks are limited by selecting issues rated B or better. They do the job with a modest expense ratio of less than 0.50 percent, one of the lowest among the fund's peers. Yields have been solidly in the 8 percent range in recent years, and a $10,000 investment a decade ago would be worth about $25,000 today. The Nicholas Income Fund is a first-class performer for the risk-averse investor.

For more information call 1-800-227-5987

TAX-EXEMPT MUNI-BOND FUNDS

VANGUARD MUNICIPALS LONG-TERM
VANGUARD MUNICIPALS INTERMEDIATE-TERM
VANGUARD MUNICIPALS SHORT-TERM
VANGUARD MUNICIPALS HIGH-YIELD

Vanguard also scored big on our SuperStar Tax-Exempt Bond Fund radar. What's the secret to their success? One of the bond fund managers, Christopher M. Ryon, gave a very simple answer: "Our shareholders own us. We do not have equity participants who have to get paid in terms of returns on equity. Our shareholders own the funds. Therefore, we can provide services to them at cost," so the margin of profit accrues directly to the fund's investors, not outside investors. In addition, you pay no loads and no commissions. On top of that, expenses are often no more than 20 percent of the competition's. And turnover is comparatively low, maximizing your after-tax returns.

Vanguard started three of these muni funds in 1977; the High-Yield fund opened a year later. Ian MacKinnon and his team have been managing this quartet for more than 10 years. The Intermediate-Term muni fund is the largest, with over $7.5 billion in assets; the Long-Term and Short-Term have about $2.5 billion between them; and the High-Yield has about $3 billion. The team runs all four funds with the same disciplined approach to generating income and preserving capital.

Securities selected for each of these four muni funds must fit its designated objectives, based on state and sector credit rating, yield-curve position, maturity, and duration, as well as economic and monetary forecasts. Consequently, the securities are 80 to 95 percent investment-grade bonds rated single-A or better. In fact, the High-Yield portfolio is a misnomer. It is not a euphemism for junk bonds; the fund merely invests in longer maturities, 15 to 25 years.

We asked Ryon what kind of investors would be interested in the three basic types of government bond funds: munis, U.S. Treasuries, and Ginnie Maes. For example, who should buy one versus the other? And what are the basic differences between them? Ryon replied:

> The first major difference would be based upon where the investor is in their life cycle. To the extent that they're at

a time where they need to focus more on income generation or shorter-term goals, they may want to go to bond funds.

Longer-term bond funds have much more stable dividend streams, but you have much more price volatility. If you're looking for a stable income generation product, you might look at a long or intermediate term bond fund.

To the extent that you have a shorter-term horizon on what these monies are to do, you may look at a money-market or a short-term bond fund.

And if you're in a higher tax bracket, you might say to yourself, OK, at this point in my life I need to allocate *x* percentage of my portfolio to bond funds. In my tax bracket, I get a better after-tax return from a municipal bond fund than I do a taxable bond fund, so I'll make the allocation to a municipal bond fund.

All four Vanguard muni funds perform well, in part thanks to Vanguard's ultra-low expense ratio of 0.19 percent—that's often a half to a full point less than the competition. Higher volatility (beta) comes with longevity, from the 0.80 to 0.90 range for the Long-Term and High-Yield, to 0.10 to 0.20 for the Short-Term. Total returns over a 10- to 15-year period are in the range of 9 to 10 percent for the Long-Term portfolio, 8 to 9 percent for Intermediate-Term, and around 5 percent for Short-Term. In the competitive arena, the Intermediate-Term and High-Yield portfolios rank consistently higher in their peer categories. If you had invested $10,000 in any one of these four winners a decade ago, today your investment would be almost $25,000 for the Long-Term and High-Yield funds, slightly less for the Intermediate-Term fund, and over $15,000 for the Short-Term fund. These are truly impressive statistics, plus you get some excellent tax advantages.

For more information call 1-800-662-7447

T. ROWE PRICE TAX-FREE HIGH-YIELD

Typical of any municipal bond fund in this category, the
T. Rowe Price High-Yield muni fund is designed to deliver
maximum current income exempt from federal income
taxes. The fund opened its doors in 1985, with manager
Steve Wolfe taking the reins in 1994. Wolfe adopts a
conservative approach to the higher risks in this corner
of the market. He does this by broadly diversifying this
$1 billion-plus fund across a wide range of credits and
states, with over 400 issues spread across the United States.

By keeping over one-third of the portfolio in investment-grade triple-A- to A-rated issues recently, rather
than lower-grade credits, Wolfe has clearly demonstrated
his strong bent toward safety. However, performance
hasn't suffered. Yields and total return have been solid
since Wolfe took charge, and well before. Total returns
are in the 8 to 9 percent range over the longer term,
slightly below the Lehman Brothers Muni Bond index
benchmark, and well ahead of the returns of the fund's
peer group. A $10,000 investment here a decade ago
would be worth almost $25,000 today. This fund is an
excellent choice for risk-tolerant investors who seek
above-average tax-exempt income.

For more information call 1-800-638-5660

STRONG HIGH-YIELD MUNICIPALS

Here's another first-class performer in the high-yield muni
arena, with over $600 million in assets. Mary-Kay Bour-
bulas has been managing the fund since 1995, 2 years
after its inception. Bourbulas is a unique deal-maker,
with over 50 percent of the fund's holdings consisting of
privately negotiated unrated issues, presumably B-rated
equivalents that improve yields.

In the quasi-entrepreneurial niche that Bourbulas has
carved out for the fund, she often picks up the entire
issue, allowing for close oversight of the credit in the

future. Maturities are in the 15- to 25-year range. Her unique investment strategy has been paying off handsomely for T. Rowe Price investors interested in tax-exempt income, with total returns ranging from 8 to 9 percent. As a result, in recent years the fund has typically beaten the high-yield muni competition, while keeping close to the Lehman Brothers Muni Bond benchmark.

For more information call 1-800-368-1030

U.S. GOVERNMENT BOND FUNDS

VANGUARD FIXED-INCOME
LONG-TERM U.S. TREASURIES

Here's the MacKinnon/Auwaerter team on the job again, this time performing their magic with guaranteed U.S. Treasury bonds. Vanguard created the fund in 1986 and Ian MacKinnon took charge in 1991. Assets are now around $1.3 billion. The fund enjoys a competitive edge similar to that of other Vanguard bond funds: In this case, a very low expense ratio of 0.27 puts the competition at a serious disadvantage before the game even begins.

As with other long-term securities funds, volatility (beta) is rather high, over 2.00 to the S&P 500, although in line with that of other long Treasuries. As for performance, the fund's total returns are in the general range of 8 to 11 percent, which helps MacKinnon's fund beat most of his peers, while tracking close to the Lehman Brothers Long Government index. A $10,000 investment a decade ago would be worth over $30,000 today.

For more information call 1-800-662-7447

VANGUARD FIXED-INCOME GNMA

Fund manager Paul Kaplan may be a relative newcomer to Vanguard's SuperStar bond team, but he's an experienced money manager with a 20-year track record, which is about as long as Vanguard's GNMA portfolio has been around. Kaplan has also been the manager of the bond side of the $25 billion Vanguard Wellington hybrid fund since 1994.

Ginnie Mae securities are backed by pools of mortgages guaranteed by the Government National Mortgage Association, a federal agency. Vanguard's fund is 100 percent loaded with triple-A-rated, no-credit-risk Ginnie Mae bonds. With over $10 billion in assets, this fund looks like a solid answer to the prayers of investors who want guaranteed income plus capital preservation

This portfolio is very conservatively managed, with expenses around 0.30 percent and turnover a low, low 3 percent. Long-term total returns are in the 8 to 10 percent range. With these figures, Vanguard's Ginnie Mae winds up beating the majority in its peer group. If you'd invested $10,000 here a decade ago, it would have grown to about $25,000 today. This is a perfect choice for investors interested in maximum guaranteed income plus capital preservation. The beauty of these Ginnie Mae funds is that a small investor can invest in them for substantially less than the required minimum of $25,000 for individual GNMA bonds.

For more information call 1-800-662-7447

STRONG GOVERNMENT SECURITIES

Here's another fine offering from the Strong family of funds. Managers Bradley Tank and John Bender operate from a solid conservative tradition, focusing on safety and risk control through solid credits. Tank has been managing this $1.3 billion fund since 1990, taking the helm 4 years after the fund's inception, with Bender joining him as comanager in 1997. Their conservative investment strategy is evident, in part, from their addition of corporate bonds to this guaranteed U.S. government bond portfolio, to the tune of 20 percent of the assets.

Government issues include a balanced mix of U.S. Treasuries and mortgage-backed bonds. Performance ranges comfortably at or above the Lehman Brothers intermediate government/corporate bond index. Moreover, with total returns hovering around 8 to 9 percent for the longer term, the Tank/Bender team outshines the competition. A $10,000 investment here a decade ago would be worth over $25,000 today. Although, at 0.80 percent, their expenses are about one-third higher than those of most no-loads in the category, so far they appear to be justifying the extra expense with superior performance.

For more information call 1-800-368-1030

AMERICAN CENTURY–BENHAM TARGET MATURITY 2020

Are you a short-term market timer? Zeros are for you. Are you a long-term, buy-and-hold investor? Zeros are for you, too! How can that be? Isn't this a big contradiction?

Zero-coupon U.S. Treasury bond funds are fascinating because, paradoxically, they do work for *both* the short-term speculator *and* the long-term investor.

American Century–Benham Target Maturity bond funds make up six of the seven such funds in existence. These zero-coupon bond funds are not a large peer group, accounting for only about $3 billion in total assets. Each of the six funds will be liquidated at maturity, in 2000, 2005, 2010, 2015, 2020, and 2025. Turnover is in the range of 20 percent. Expenses are just 0.60 percent. Average annual returns have been 10 percent in the past decade. But don't be fooled; volatility is high. Back in 1994, returns were a negative 17 percent, followed by 60 percent-plus returns the following year.

Volatility (beta) is over four times higher with such funds than the S&P 500—that's right, four times higher. This fund will rocket up four times as high as the S&P

on an upturn, and plummet four times as low on a down-turn!

Zero-coupon bond funds are obviously not for the squeamish. In the short run, zeros are a pure roller-coaster ride. Owning them may be too nerve-wracking for anyone with a low threshold for the pain that goes along with wild market swings. However, if you are a patient, long-term investor, you can buy a par value $1,000 zero-coupon bond for only $20 and be absolutely certain that Uncle Sam will pay you at maturity. And you can expect virtually the same guaranteed returns and payoff from a zero-coupon bond fund.

How much would a $10,000 investment in one of these funds a decade ago be worth today? The longer maturities, with their higher volatility, are worth more: Target 2000 grew to slightly over $25,000 in the last decade. During the same period Target 2005 grew to around $30,000; Target 2010, to almost $40,000; and Target 2015, to more than $45,000. So if you'd had the stomach for the volatility, you'd have been justly rewarded—eventually. The bottom line, however, is that these funds are not for the average buy-and-hold investor.

For more information call 1-800-345-2021

PART

How to
Build a
SUPERSTAR
PORTFOLIO

ERE COMES the fun part. Now you're going to put together the information from Parts 1 and 2 and build a winning portfolio. You'll see the ten principles from Part 1 in action. You'll discover how many successful individual investors are already picking the SuperStar Funds from Part 2. You'll also learn how to apply a few basic rules in creating the right portfolio for your particular needs. Let me say first, however, that no two investors' or families' financial needs are identical, so use the examples here to help you construct the right portfolio; but don't be afraid to make adjustments for your specific needs and requirements.

SECTION 18: DISCOVERING YOUR ASSET ALLOCATIONS

IN THIS SECTION I'LL review the not-so-secret formula for building a successful portfolio—structuring the right asset allocations for your particular life-style demands. As I've mentioned (and might again), your asset allocations account for over 90 percent of your portfolio's returns; so choose wisely, and stick to them.

SECTION 19: REAL PEOPLE, REAL PORTFOLIOS

THIS SECTION WILL present specific examples of how some savvy investors are successfully putting their portfolios in order, along with discussions of some of the problems and challenges they've encountered along the way. I use real people, and real-life examples, to demonstrate that you, as a smart individual investor, can manage a simple portfolio of funds on your own. I selected these particular examples because they fit a wide variety of life-styles, age groups, goals, and time-to-need patterns, and they should give you some ideas of what will work for you.

We'll look at a starter kit for beginning investors—those just getting their feet wet; millionaires-in-training—how a young married couple in their early 30s has adopted an aggressive stance on the way to early retirement; and the process of balancing multiple goals—advice for families with many competing needs, including buying a home, saving for the children's college education, and preparing for their own retirement. Plus, a new boomer tells how he manages his portfolio in five minutes a day, without professional advice, as does an aggressive 75-year-old retiree who's dealing with inflation. You might just see yourself in some of these examples.

SECTION 20:
PORTFOLIO ALTERNATIVES:
OUT OF THE BOX

HERE I'LL LOOK AT several interesting opportunities for investors, including DRIPs, socially responsible investing, and index portfolios. You'll find a lot of promising ideas in this section, ones I hope will offer you something new that you hadn't considered before. Of course, only some will make sense for your particular needs. They're here to show you alternatives beyond your normal range of experience. As my mentors have often said, take what works for you now, file the rest away for future reference, and move on to the next adventure.

SECTION 21: REBALANCING
RULES: HOW TO MONITOR
YOUR PORTFOLIO

TIME MARCHES ON, and so do the financial markets. And time has a way of changing the game and the playing field, sometimes quickly, sometimes slowly. As a result, a few months or a year from now the funds in your portfolio will have either increased or declined in value. You'll also be adding new money and reinvesting your returns, so you'll need to rebalance your portfolio. Here, almost the last word, are rules that will help you successfully rethink your investments and keep you focused on the right asset allocations.

Discovering Your Asset Allocations

THE KEY TO BUILDING a winning mutual fund portfolio is your asset allocations, not the funds you pick.

FOR THE VAST MAJORITY of individual investors, the key to a successful mutual fund portfolio is selecting the right asset allocations. If you learn only one thing from this book, please remember this. In fact, as you've already discovered, research studies have confirmed that over 90 percent—that's right, 90 percent—of the success of any mutual fund portfolio is directly related to asset categories and not the specific funds you pick. Financial professionals who sell, manage, and rate specific funds might deny this, but it's one of the core strategies that guides most objective planners and advisers in the business.

This is why I put so much emphasis on creating and monitoring a personal financial plan *first*. To be sure, picking the right funds will always be important—but only after you develop your portfolio's asset allocations using your personal financial plan. After that, you must exercise the discipline and vigilance to adhere to those allocations, rather than chasing advice you read this week or next month about hot funds in the news.

Think of investing as a long-distance sport that demands endurance: Financial planning is analogous to all your preseason training, your game plans, and every pregame warm-up session. All this prep work is absolutely essential before you step onto the field and actually play the first game of the season—in this case, investing. Pre-planning leads to a winning portfolio.

THE BIG SECRET
THE MEDIA AND FUND
COMPANIES WON'T TELL YOU

UNFORTUNATELY, YOU MAY not hear asset allocations emphasized often enough. The reasons for this oversight are quite understandable:

◆ First: many investment professionals don't want you to believe research results such as Brinson's report. They're out to convince you that their particular funds are superior, that they are the best stock-pickers, and that they know your financial needs better than even you do. Their ad pitches are designed to drown out the simple fact that, as Brinson has proven, your asset-allocation decisions, not the particular funds you pick, account for over 90 percent of your return.

◆ Second: the financial press thrives on hot news—the top funds of the week, the best managers of the month, the best stocks of the day. By contrast, asset allocation is as boring as the pregame warm-up for the championship. As a former newspaper editor and television executive, I know how great the pressures are on the news media to create a sense of urgency (often when one doesn't really exist) in order to grab the audience's attention.

In short, the press and media are guilty of short-term thinking. In spite of what they say, they thrive on creating a feeling of immediacy and a need to act now—today. Of course, because many media companies are publicly held, they are heavily influenced by their own quarterly earnings reports and bonuses. So the reality for you and your family is that you must take charge of your own financial needs and your own bottom line—or someone else will do it for you.

BUILDING A SUCCESSFUL FUND PORTFOLIO

IN SUMMARY, here are four simple rules to help you put your asset allocation planning in the context of an overall investment strategy:

1 Prepare a financial plan. Another reason I keep emphasizing this point is simply because—surprise, surprise—too many investors don't do enough planning or saving and, therefore, they are unprepared for the future. You need a plan.

2 Save on a regular schedule. Research studies indicate quite clearly that today's average investors are only saving about one-third of what they'll need for retirement or any other goal. If this describes you, change the pattern. Make sure you're above the average, more like 10 percent than 3 percent. Regular savings are essential. Clearly, the trick is to plan your savings in accordance with the goals that are identified in your financial plan.

3 Stick with your portfolio's asset allocations. Don't jump ship every time you hear the press making noise about a short-term correction—because you will hear those hints often. The market will have bad days (and weeks or months). Assuming you're one of the new, enlightened breed of responsible, do-it-yourself investors, you know that long-term investing is the way to go. So stick with your allocations. Review and rebalance your portfolio as needed.

4 Stop chasing hot-funds-of-the-week. Avoid the temptation of constantly chasing after the latest, hottest, multi-starred fund or the well-marketed darling fund manager being hyped by the financial press. If you give in to the hype, you might expose your portfolio to higher risks, usually at the expense of the overall asset allocations developed using your financial planning tools in the first step above. Also, if you are a fund "trader" you'll pay substantially higher fees than if you choose the right portfolio the first time.

A KEEP-IT-SIMPLE STRATEGIC MODEL

CREATING A SUCCESSFUL portfolio—one that works for your particular life-style and family needs—is really quite simple, as the accompanying chart suggests. I'm assuming you've made the crucial first step and that you're saving regularly according to your financial plan. Next, focus on the time you have to invest and on your asset allocations. Then you can improve your position by picking ten winning funds. But the bottom line is that if you save regularly and you buy funds that fit your asset-allocation mix, you will do as well as, or better than, most professionals in the financial world. Yes, it's really that simple.

In Part 1 we discussed a range of five model portfolios—let's revisit them in greater detail now. I list a range of five models here, but I could have used the same formula to create just three model portfolios, or ten portfolios, that fit along this same continuum. What's impor-

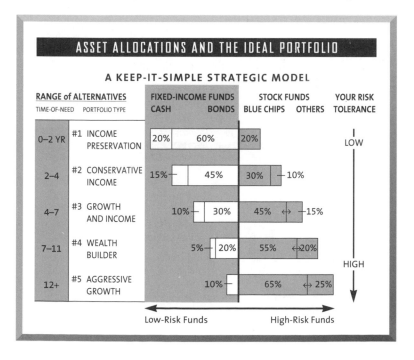

ASSET ALLOCATIONS AND THE IDEAL PORTFOLIO

A KEEP-IT-SIMPLE STRATEGIC MODEL

RANGE of ALTERNATIVES		FIXED-INCOME FUNDS		STOCK FUNDS		YOUR RISK
TIME-OF-NEED	PORTFOLIO TYPE	CASH	BONDS	BLUE CHIPS	OTHERS	TOLERANCE
0–2 YR	#1 INCOME PRESERVATION	20%	60%	20%		LOW
2–4	#2 CONSERVATIVE INCOME	15%	45%	30%	10%	
4–7	#3 GROWTH AND INCOME	10%	30%	45%	15%	
7–11	#4 WEALTH BUILDER	5%	20%	55%	20%	
12+	#5 AGGRESSIVE GROWTH		10%	65%	25%	HIGH

Low-Risk Funds ←——————→ High-Risk Funds

tant is that you narrow it down to just one that works for your unique needs. These should get you started.

WINNING PORTFOLIO #1: INCOME PRESERVATION

The "Income Preservation" portfolio is designed for investors with fairly immediate financial needs, usually less than two years, and/or those with a very low tolerance for market risk and volatility. This portfolio relies heavily on fixed-income funds—bond funds, hybrid funds, and money-market funds. Stock funds that fit this model would most likely be solid blue-chip growth funds with regular dividends.

Stability of current income and minimum risk of capital loss are of prime importance in an Income Preservation portfolio. Growth and capital appreciation are not. And the timing of investors' withdrawal needs is more important than their chronological age. As a result, an Income Preservation portfolio may well be just as appropriate for a 65-year-old retiree as for a twenty-something grad student, assuming either one needs steady income and wants to minimize the risk of losing precious capital.

Here are recommended percentages of the types of funds from Part 2 that fit this portfolio model. You can go back and select the specific funds that fit your needs:

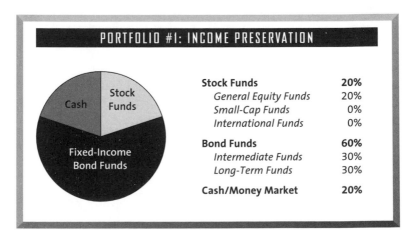

PORTFOLIO #1: INCOME PRESERVATION

Stock Funds	**20%**
General Equity Funds	20%
Small-Cap Funds	0%
International Funds	0%
Bond Funds	**60%**
Intermediate Funds	30%
Long-Term Funds	30%
Cash/Money Market	**20%**

WINNING PORTFOLIO #2: CONSERVATIVE INCOME

The "Conservative Income" portfolio is also designed for investors who require a steady income flow. However, these investors also want some growth and capital appreciation. Since such investors have at least two to four years before they need the money, they're willing to take some modest risks, although probably few.

Investors with this relatively short-term time frame and a higher risk tolerance may consider some higher-risk stock funds. However, big-cap, blue-chip funds are the safer, more likely choice. The Conservative Income model may be right for families saving to buy a new home in the relatively near future.

Again, here are recommended percentages of types of funds from Part 2 that fit this portfolio model. You can go back to Part 2 and select the specific funds that work for you:

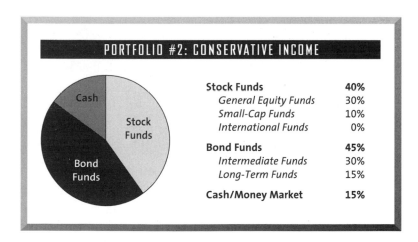

PORTFOLIO #2: CONSERVATIVE INCOME	
Stock Funds	**40%**
General Equity Funds	30%
Small-Cap Funds	10%
International Funds	0%
Bond Funds	**45%**
Intermediate Funds	30%
Long-Term Funds	15%
Cash/Money Market	**15%**

WINNING PORTFOLIO #3: GROWTH AND INCOME

This "Growth and Income" portfolio is structured for investors who want capital appreciation and don't need immediate income from their portfolio. Their tolerance for risk is moderate, and they often have a medium-term time horizon of five to seven years, which is longer than an average bull/bear market cycle. These investors are willing to ride out near-term market fluctuations in search of reasonably solid growth and capital appreciation.

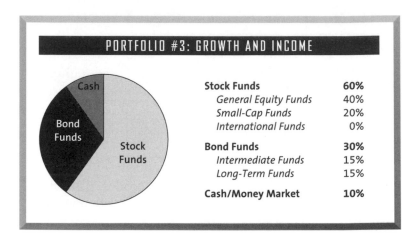

PORTFOLIO #3: GROWTH AND INCOME

Stock Funds	**60%**
General Equity Funds	40%
Small-Cap Funds	20%
International Funds	0%
Bond Funds	**30%**
Intermediate Funds	15%
Long-Term Funds	15%
Cash/Money Market	**10%**

Conservative investors with this time frame should put most of their stock allocation in large-cap, blue-chip funds. Investors with a higher tolerance for risk would select a higher allocation of aggressive-growth and small-cap, global, and even some sector funds. This portfolio may work for families putting aside money for a home or for a teenage child's college education.

WINNING PORTFOLIO #4: WEALTH BUILDER
The "Wealth Builder" portfolio is designed for long-term investors seeking strong growth and appreciation in their portfolios. Because the time horizon of these investors is seven to eleven years, and possibly more, they are more interested in building future wealth than realizing current income. Returns are systematically reinvested.

This is a fairly aggressive portfolio, for mature couples planning ahead for retirement or young couples saving for their young children's college education. Investors with this time frame and a higher tolerance for risk may be willing to invest a larger percentage of their stock allocation in aggressive-growth, small-cap, sector, or global funds, rather than blue-chip domestic stocks. Keep in mind, however, that statistics show that blue-chip funds offer returns fairly comparable to these alternatives, and with less risk. In fact, about two-thirds of all stock fund assets are in the middle-of-the-road growth, equity-income, and growth and income peer groups.

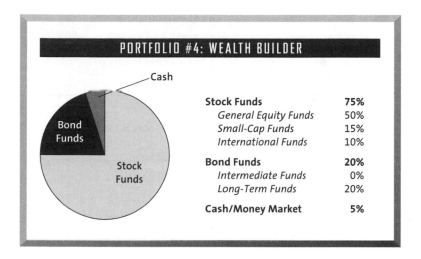

PORTFOLIO #4: WEALTH BUILDER

Cash

Bond Funds

Stock Funds

Stock Funds	**75%**
General Equity Funds	50%
Small-Cap Funds	15%
International Funds	10%
Bond Funds	**20%**
Intermediate Funds	0%
Long-Term Funds	20%
Cash/Money Market	**5%**

WINNING PORTFOLIO #5: AGGRESSIVE GROWTH

The "Aggressive Growth" portfolio is designed for an investor with a long-term horizon (a decade or more), plus patience and a strong tolerance for short-term risks and market fluctuations. Current income is not important.

These investors are responsible and disciplined, building portfolios for maximum long-term growth. They are willing to accept a high degree of risk and near-term volatility, while aggressively pursuing higher returns for the long haul.

The more risk-tolerant investors may buy a larger portion of aggressive-growth and small-cap, sector, and global funds. These investors are planning ahead for retirement, are very knowledgeable about investing, devote a reasonable amount of time to staying on top of the markets, and enjoy the game of investing.

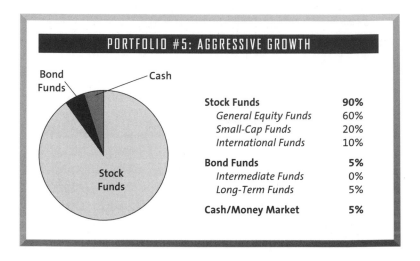

PORTFOLIO #5: AGGRESSIVE GROWTH

Stock Funds	**90%**
General Equity Funds	60%
Small-Cap Funds	20%
International Funds	10%
Bond Funds	**5%**
Intermediate Funds	0%
Long-Term Funds	5%
Cash/Money Market	**5%**

A KEEP-IT-SIMPLE FORMULA
THAT WORKS FOR EVERYONE

HOW CAN YOU STRUCTURE an ideal portfolio? It's simple. First, focus less on your age and more on your goals and on when you need the money. After all, you could be 16 or 65 but still have a short-term horizon for when you'll need to cash in your funds. For example:

◆ A retiree looking forward to 20 to 30 years of healthy life is a long-term investor.

◆ However, a 20-year-old with immediate college expenses has a strong need for short-term capital preservation.

When you need the money defines your risk tolerance—how much you can afford to lose. The longer the time left for investing, the more you can afford to ride through many short-term ups and downs in the market. It's all about your unique "time-of-need."

Look at the chart "Asset Allocations and the Ideal Portfolio" on page 173. The longer you have to your time-of-need, the more risk you can assume with your investments. For example, look at the lower part of the chart: If you have 7 to 11 years, or 12 or more, you can tolerate more risk on the downside in order to generate higher upside returns. Certainly most investors under 50 years old who are building a long-term retirement portfolio automatically fall into this category.

However, if you have much shorter-term needs—such as a planned home purchase, medical payments, or retirement living expenses—you should look at the top part of the chart, showing that a higher percentage of your money should be in lower-return fixed-income funds and money markets, because they also have much less downside risk. Obviously, knowing your own personal tolerance for risk will help you fine-tune your asset allocation. But generally speaking, your time-of-need will control the decision more than your chronological age.

Before I move on to some interesting real-life examples, please remember that our "one-size-fits-all" portfolios in this section are only starting points. Above all, remember to utilize the ten principles in Part 1 as you create your financial plan and choose the asset allocations that suit your needs.

Real People, Real Portfolios

HERE'S A SNAPSHOT of several very different people with distinct needs, and a look at how each is planning an investment portfolio that works for his or her unique life-style.

WHAT'S THE BEST WAY TO get started investing in mutual funds? By this point you should realize that my first advice is always to take the time to devise a long-term financial plan. It's worth the time and effort. It's essential.

A STARTER KIT: ADVICE FOR NEW INVESTORS JUST TESTING THE WATERS

A TWENTY-SOMETHING investor who is just getting started will, it's pretty safe to assume, have a twenty-year-plus time horizon and an all-equity portfolio. This approach can also work for a baby boomer getting a late start who must balance safety with growth. But if you happen to need the money sooner than ten years, begin adding in bond funds and gradually increasing the percentage allocation as you draw closer to the time you need the money.

The key for new investors' success is to get into the game and *just do it . . . start building your portfolio today.*

This book is a great starting point for new investors. But don't stop here with your investment education. It's an ongoing process that requires hands-on, on-the-job experience to succeed. There are some additional resources that you should consult on a regular basis if you're planning to get serious about your investments. In recent years I've recommended *Kiplinger's Mutual Funds,* an annual publication sold on newsstands each February through May, as the one magazine to buy if you're buying only one fund magazine all year. No computers are necessary here. You'll get a simple outline of the major steps in their suggested process, complete with worksheets and easy-to-use savings and risk calculators.

Three other must-subscribe print magazines for mutual fund gurus-in-training are *Mutual Funds, Money,* and *Kiplinger's Personal Finance Magazine.* Monthly coverage includes virtually every possible subject you could conceive of in the funds world. You might get hooked on these three.

If you finish this book and also devour the magazines above, forge ahead: There's a lot of very good, easily accessible print information to satisfy your appetite for financial knowledge. Check the Resources section of this book for a comprehensive listing.

MODEL PORTFOLIOS

THE "STARTER KIT" model portfolio that best fits a new investor with a long-term horizon is the basic long-term portfolio. It can be used as a starting point for designing your first portfolio or to set up an IRA or your 401(k) while you are still exploring this new area of investing.

BASIC LONG-TERM STARTER PORTFOLIO, 10+ YEARS

◆ 30% index funds from Section 16
◆ 25% blue-chip stock funds from Section 11
◆ 15% small-cap funds from Section 12
◆ 10% global funds from Section 13
◆ 10% sector funds from Section 14
◆ 10% hybrid funds from Section 15

Once you get closer to your goals—for example, into the 7- to 10-year range—start downshifting using this portfolio scenario: Add in a bond fund (20 percent) and you may proportionately reduce the other four funds.

BASIC SHORT-TERM STARTER PORTFOLIO, 4 TO 7 YEARS

◆ 30% blue-chip stock funds from Section 11
◆ 20% fixed-income funds from Section 17
◆ 25% hybrid funds from Section 15
◆ 15% index funds from Section 16
◆ 5% small-cap funds from Section 12
◆ 5% global funds from Section 13

Now let's look at some examples of investors who have different needs and are constructing portfolios that will grow with them. These are the average investors-next-door who gave us the opportunity to study and critique their investments.

EXAMPLE #1:
MILLIONAIRES-IN-TRAINING

Only 30, aggressive, disciplined savers, and planning to retire early. . . .

"FINANCIAL MAGAZINES, if not their readers, are in danger of forgetting that their subject can be fun," noted *Worth* magazine's editor in a lighter moment. Well, here's a young couple in their early 30s who must be having a lot of fun, judging from the portfolio they're putting together. Like many of the others in this section, Sam and his wife Sarah sent us their financial plans for review and comment. Fortunately, if these savvy young investors keep up the good work, they should be able to retire in style—early if they choose. They've heard all the scary news about the shortfall in Social Security and company pension programs. They're clearly taking charge of their own future and doing it like pros. Here's what Sam and Sarah already have as investments, building toward a solid future:

◆ Mutual funds, $100,000
◆ Stocks, $110,000
◆ Cash, $20,000
◆ Bonds, $0
◆ Total portfolio, $230,000

That's right: They're only in their thirties and already have almost a cool quarter of a million dollars, with about half in stocks rather than funds. And time is definitely in their favor. They're on the way to becoming millionaires a few times over by the time they reach retirement.

Don't beat yourself up if you haven't saved as much or started as early as this couple. Starting from scratch— even if nothing were set aside, as is the case with many young people raising families—Sam would need to save only $750 a month to build a $1 million nest egg by age 65. But if you *are* like Sam and Sarah, congratulate yourself and keep up the diligence. Everything is in their favor.

Let's look at what they have going for them and see if we can draw some conclusions. We'll assume they intend to wait another 30 years before retiring in their early 60s:

1 Reinvesting. The $230,000 they already have will grow automatically with reinvesting and appreciation, *even if they add no new money*. This, of course, assumes there are no withdrawals. If they can earn 10 percent and reinvest dividends, their portfolio will double every 5 to 6 years. So they'll easily have more than $1 million by the time they retire in 30 years.

2 Steady additions. If Sam and Sarah also kick in new money, another $1,000 each month for the next 30 years, and if they keep investing the money as they have been, they'll be millionaires a few times over. In fact, they will be able to retire well before their 60s if they set their minds to it and continue investing wisely.

3 Market cycles. With 30 years to go before retirement, Sam and Sarah should expect to ride through the ups and downs of perhaps five market cycles—five bulls up and five bears down, one full cycle every 4 years on average.

LOOKING AT THE ASSET ALLOCATIONS

In many ways, these investors don't really need to be told how to choose funds—not because they won't need some advice from time to time, but because they're already on the right track and, more importantly, because they need to develop confidence in their ability to control their own financial destiny. Just look at the specific funds (the percentages for the main headings are their fund asset-allocation percentages; the percentages next to each fund are the 3-year average annual returns for all the funds at that time, except PBHG Technology & Communications and Guinness Small-Cap, which at the time were one-year returns):

Growth and Aggressive Growth (20% of portfolio)

◆ Oakmark Fund (25.1% return)
◆ Baron Asset (28.9%)
◆ Fasciano Fund (26.0%)
◆ Vanguard Index Growth (31.8%)

Sector Funds (42% of portfolio)

◆ PBHG Technology & Communications (34.0% return)
◆ Interactive Investment Technology Value (57.1%)
◆ Invesco Strategic Financial Services (33.3%)
◆ Invesco Strategic Health Sciences (28.8%)
◆ Fidelity Real Estate Invest (22.6%)

Global Funds (38% of portfolio)

◆ Mutual Discovery Z (24.2% return)
◆ Fidelity New Markets Income (20.0%)
◆ Guinness Flight China & Hong Kong (15.0%)
◆ Guinness Flight Asia Small-Cap (20.4%)

Great portfolio, but are thirteen funds too many? Some financial planners say yes. Investors get very little additional diversification for their risk after ten funds—

and I recommend sticking with ten. But with multiple IRAs and 401(k) plans, plus taxable accounts, thirteen funds isn't something to fret about if you're picking winners.

At the time I reviewed Sam and Sarah's portfolio, over half of the funds were already on our SuperStar Funds directory with five in their respective top-ten lists and one in the top twenty. Their 3-year returns range from a low of 24.2 percent to a high of 33.3 percent. These included Oakmark, Baron Asset, Fasciano, Vanguard Index Growth, Invesco Strategic Financial, Invesco Strategic Health Sciences, and Mutual Discovery Z.

The other six funds are also solid choices: PBHG Technology & Communications, Interactive Investment Technology Value, Fidelity Real Estate Invest, and Fidelity New Markets Income. Guinness Flight China & Hong Kong and Guinness Flight Asia Small-Cap have since dropped.

A few of these funds didn't show up on our Super-Star radar simply because they're new or for some other screening reason: PBHG Technology & Communications and Guinness Flight Asia Small-Cap lacked 3-year returns. And the relatively new Interactive Investment Technology Value only appeared on one "best funds" list I monitored at the time, in spite of its phenomenal 57 percent first-year return.

MUTUAL FUND ASSET ALLOCATIONS: AGGRESSIVE, SECTORS, AND GLOBAL

What about the asset allocations for the funds in this portfolio, exclusive of cash and stocks? Here's the mix:
◆ Growth and aggressive growth (20%)
◆ Sector funds (42%)
◆ Global funds (38%)

Most model financial plans and planning tools would caution that the global funds are too high at 38 percent, that 15 to 25 percent makes more sense. However, since Sam and Sarah have $110,000 in stocks and $20,000 in cash, their funds constitute less than half of their total investment portfolio, so their global fund holdings appear reasonable. In addition, after the Asia crisis, Sam and Sarah needed to rebalance and move funds into the developed countries in Europe or into domestic equities, taking advantage of the tax losses on the Asia funds.

Generally speaking, investing as much as 42 percent may also be too heavy, but it's hard to find fault given their choices. Their sector funds are in technology, financial, health care, and real estate, all growth areas in our economy and also favorites among professional money managers.

Sam also added these comments: "I have fifteen individual stocks in a taxable account totaling $110,000; just over half of these are technology or communications related; the others are consumer, financial, or gaming/hotel stocks. Since my individual picks are not diversified by design, I use the mutual funds to get some limited diversity within a sector. I add to this account on a regular basis. I usually hold stocks for 1 to 3 years, but have several that I've held for 3 to 5 years. I also have about $20,000 in cash or money-market accounts at any given time." With that much cash, he might consider an ultra-short-term bond fund like Strong Advantage to increase his returns a couple of points without adding much risk.

Assuming the decisions in their stock portfolio are as well thought out as their funds, Sam and Sarah don't have much to worry about in the long run. After a detailed review, some financial planners might say they've got too much in sectors and global, and perhaps not enough in blue chips. But they are apparently savvy enough to know that and are more than adequately diversified, with thirteen funds and fifteen stocks in their portfolio spread across several solid sectors and styles.

EXAMPLE #2: FAMILIES
WITH MULTIPLE GOALS

Late bloomers taking charge, getting aggressive. . . .

HERE'S A PORTFOLIO FOR families who have several goals at once, like saving to buy a home and paying for their children's college education.

Harry's a latecomer to the investment world, a 42-year-old teacher who says he "can't rely on his teacher's retirement plan or Social Security." Although both will provide some support in the future, "it is up to me to try to build a nest egg to supplement my retirement." Here's the game plan he asked us to comment on, as he juggles several goals and needs with different time frames.

Harry has two children just starting junior high. He plans to work about 20 years more, perhaps longer if his kids need the money for college. On the one hand, a horizon of 15 years to retirement makes him a long-term investor for purposes of retirement. However, as a responsible father with children less than 6 years away from college, he fits a different profile. But the parental role is more immediate and likely to take first priority in his planning. Thus, he has a relatively short-term, conservative investment horizon.

For other families, buying a new home may also be part of their financial planning, especially during the earlier phases of their life cycle. The reality is that most families are in such complex situations, faced with multiple goals, and should analyze all their separate accounts as a single portfolio with an overall financial plan.

The Merrill Lynch Boomer Retirement Index annually warns the 76 million Americans born between 1946 and 1962 that they are saving only one-third (about 34 percent) of what they'll need to retire in the life-style they're used to. Harry admits he started late, but he's clearly committed to a solid program of regular, disciplined saving and investing. He made a mistake a number of years ago and said that he got burned on a "fund scam." As a result of that experience, he has been a very conservative investor until recently, when he sold some accounts and consolidated the rest. After the consolidation, Harry has a total of $150,000 stashed away.

Right off the bat he deserves a high score, because many of his contemporaries have small or no nest eggs. So our hats are off to Harry and his family. He's a responsible boomer with respectable savings and time left to triple his assets or better.

LOOKING AT THE ASSET ALLOCATIONS

Here's the portfolio of mutual funds Harry created when he consolidated his accounts. He also has a couple of small stock holdings that equal about 3 percent of his portfolio. Average 3-year annual returns then current are shown:

Janus Fund Family
◆ Janus Fund (22.0%)
◆ Janus Enterprise (15.0%)
◆ Janus Mercury (22.3%)
◆ Janus Worldwide (21.9%)
◆ Janus Overseas (22.8%)

T. Rowe Price Fund Family
◆ T. Rowe Equity Income (24.3%)
◆ T. Rowe Price Mid-Cap (25.7%)

American Funds
◆ Washington Mutual Investors (27.1%)

Stein Roe Farnham
◆ Stein Roe Special (20.0%)

Money-Market Account
◆ Schwab MoneyMarket/IRA

Harry says he's a late-blooming boomer, yet he's obviously taking his responsibilities seriously, both as a parent and as an eventual retiree. He has a savings plan, and one hopes he's setting aside a minimum of 10 percent of his income monthly in the family nest egg. About half of the funds were SuperStars at the time this portfolio was presented. Fortunately, 92 percent of his portfolio is protected in tax-deferred accounts, although he should consider increasing other accounts and creating a specific college fund for the children.

Here are a few additional observations about Harry's portfolio:

1 Consult a planner. Because Harry is getting a somewhat late start and because he has complex needs, he could accelerate his learning curve with some professional help, either from an independent financial planner or through a no-load fund family. This book is about being able to do it yourself, but it's also about using common sense and getting help when needed.

2 Add some bond funds. Why are there no fixed-income funds in Harry's portfolio? With his relatively short-term needs and the market continuing to tempt fate and the bear, Harry should review and rebalance his portfolio's asset allocations, not just run scared, chasing high returns that may have higher risks. Even the huge $3 trillion pension fund industry is cutting back on stocks, although external market conditions should not be the deciding factor for him.

An investor with a 15-year horizon before retirement may be able to ride through a few more bull/bear cycles. But Harry also has short-term needs to plan for, namely putting two teenagers through college. Someone with that profile should also be shifting the college-fund portion of the portfolio to perhaps 30 percent in bonds or bond funds, and gradually increasing it to 60 to 70 percent by the time the kids enter college.

3 Focus on fund families. Like many investors, Harry invests through a few fund families. His four Janus funds are 28 percent of his portfolio. Another 35 percent are American Funds. And 28 percent is invested with Schwab. That's a total of 91 percent concentrated with just three fund families—not an uncommon concentration today. Loyalty to a single fund family is likely to increase as fund families continue to grow considerably and add funds to create a full spectrum satisfying all investor needs and goals. With the rise in popularity of the fund supermarkets—like Fidelity FundsNetwork, Jack White's No-Fee Network, and Schwab's Mutual Fund OneSource—Harry should also consider the alternative of picking and managing his funds through one of these supermarkets.

Overall, Harry's doing a great job—he's certainly headed in the right direction, considering the investment challenges he faced earlier.

EXAMPLE #3:
A DO-IT-YOURSELF INVESTOR

He manages his portfolio in just 5 minutes a day....

A SOLID MEMBER OF America's new club of high-tech investors, Wayne is a 55-year-old engineer who is married and planning to retire in 5 to 7 years. Even at 55, his life expectancy is at least 30 more years, long enough to need a long-term investing perspective. Here's how he describes his investing strategy and process:

> I spend about 5 minutes a day on my investments. I have a spreadsheet set up with all my holdings, and I download the day's prices and import them into the spreadsheet. That's how I automatically keep track of my asset allocation, my net worth, etc.

Every weekend, I archive the week's closing prices. I use the *Wall Street Journal* to input the daily advances, declines, [and] S&P 500 prices, and update two charts: the 10-day ratio of advances to declines plotted against the S&P 500, and the advance/decline line plotted against the S&P 500. It takes about 15 minutes.

Once I'm satisfied with the asset allocation and fund selection, there isn't much to do. In fact, I have to keep myself from fiddling with it. It's like watching grass grow.

Wayne focuses first on getting the right asset allocations, before picking his funds. Resist the temptation to screw up your portfolio by thinking you're a market guru who can time the market and engage in short-term trading. Stick to a buy-and-hold strategy, then go out and play tennis, hike, or go to a movie. And avoid tampering with your portfolio too often. In fact, on many days 5 minutes may be too long; forget short-term market swings and news flashes.

LOOKING AT THE ASSET ALLOCATIONS

Wayne has twelve funds in his portfolio (and one small-cap stock), providing solid diversification. As it turns out, eight of his funds were SuperStar Funds at the time. Four of the funds are in his employer's tax-deferred 401(k) plan, equaling about 40 percent of total assets. Their then-current 3-year average annual returns are included in parentheses. His portfolio looks like this:

Conservative Equity Funds, $140,000
(55% of porfolio)
◆ Vanguard Asset Allocation (26.0% return)
◆ Heartland Value Plus (28.5%)
◆ Janus Balanced (20.7%)
◆ AS Fixed-Income Fund (7.98%)
◆ Employer-managed balanced fund 401(k)

Aggressive Domestic Equity Funds, $75,000 (30% of portfolio)

- Fidelity Low-Priced Stock (25.8%)
- Vanguard Healthcare (31.1%)
- Invesco Select Technology (26.5%)
- Vanguard Standard and Poor's 500 Index (30.3%)
- O'Shaughnessy Cornerstone Growth (new)

Aggressive Global Equity Funds, $40,000 (15% of portfolio)

- Janus Worldwide (21.8%)
- EuroPacific Growth Fund (12.1%)

This portfolio is definitely a winner: Eight of his twelve funds were SuperStar Funds, and eight of the funds, including a quarter that Wayne classified as conservative, had average annualized returns of between 21 and 31 percent at that time. He's an excellent fund-picker. The portfolio is also well diversified between conservative and aggressive, large-cap and small-cap, and domestic and foreign funds.

Moreover, for a 55-year-old family man approaching retirement, he's already sharply focused on shifting to a more conservative asset-allocation strategy with bond and hybrid funds.

Note also Wayne's rule of thumb: The percentage of "conservative" funds should equal his age. Here it's 55 percent. This benchmark is used by many investors to determine the percentage of their portfolio best kept in conservative investments such as fixed-income, hybrid, and money-market funds. Of course, the percentage will shift even more in the coming years as Wayne pursues capital preservation and avoids riskier aggressive funds. For example, at 75 years he should have 75 percent of his portfolio in conservative funds, although the 75-year-old retiree in Example #5 would disagree vigorously.

This is an impressive portfolio, in terms of both funds and strategy. Wayne spends just 5 minutes a day visiting his investments and using a spreadsheet to analyze returns. If you want more than a spreadsheet, many excellent portfolio-management systems are now available free with easy-to-use on-line investment accounts.

EXAMPLE #4:
DOWNSHIFTING FOR RETIREMENT

For investors planning to retire in the next 5 years. . . .

CLINT IS 55 YEARS OLD and plans to retire from government service in 5 years. He says he won't need to cash in investments for 6 to 9 years.

Clint has already built a portfolio with the following eight stock mutual funds, a money-market fund, and a tax-deferred 401(k) program that's tied to the S&P 500. The percentages are the actual allocation of each fund in his portfolio:

Growth Funds (30% of portfolio)
◆ American Century Value (4%)
◆ Neuberger & Berman Guardian (6%)
◆ Mutual Beacon Fund (15%)
◆ Strong Schafer Value (5%)

Aggressive Growth (20% of portfolio)
◆ American Century Ultra Fund (9%)
◆ Janus Mercury (6%)
◆ PBHG Growth (5%)

Global Fund (5% of portfolio)
◆ Janus Worldwide

Money Market (7% of portfolio)
◆ Strong Muni Money Fund

Tax-Deferred 401(k) (37% of portfolio)
◆ S&P 500 Index Fund

This is a rather aggressive portfolio, with 75 to 90 percent in stock funds, if we include the 37 percent in the employer-sponsored retirement plan. Clint has no bond funds. Moreover, 58 percent of his portfolio is in tax-deferred retirement programs: the 401(k) account, plus Neuberger & Berman Guardian and Mutual Beacon in his IRAs. As a fund-picker, Clint gets an A+ for selecting a solid collection of eight great funds for his portfolio. Consider these observations:

◆ **Three-year average returns.** Every one of Clint's eight stock funds has an average annual return of over 20 percent. The highest, PBHG Growth, has a return of 25.4 percent for the last 3 years. The lowest, Mutual Beacon Fund, showed a still-respectable 20.6 percent return at the time of this review. By contrast, if Clint had been in an index fund the past 3 years, such as Vanguard Index 500, his average annual returns would have been 28.1 percent. Clint is doing quite well considering that 90 percent of all actively managed funds fall short of the major market indexes.

◆ **SuperStar Funds.** Clint also managed to pick six SuperStar Funds out of the eight stock funds in his portfolio, and each was selected before our new SuperStar Funds directory was published. Whatever tools he is using—whether hi-tech analytics or low-tech pencil-and-paper analysis using the financial press plus gut instinct—Clint's fund-picking results certainly *look* as if he was using the SuperStar Funds directory! Moreover, Clint obviously has a talent for picking the best of the best. It turns out that 50 percent of the funds in his stock portfolio were in their SuperStar peer group.

Here are some specific observations about his investments:

1 Consider rebalancing. Clint asked whether he should sell PBHG Growth (21.5 percent) and Janus Mercury (22.4 percent) and reinvest the proceeds in two other funds, also shown here with their 3-year returns: Legg Mason Value Primary (37.1 percent) and Strong Growth

Fund (28.0 percent). Fortunately, both have 3-year returns higher than those of any of the funds in Clint's portfolio.

Clint's portfolio rebalancing seems quite natural for a 55-year-old nearing retirement. The two funds he may sell are more aggressively managed than the two growth funds he is considering buying. Generally, however, Clint's decision may merely fine-tune what is otherwise a solid, winning portfolio without adding much value. Remember: Avoid tinkering unnecessarily. But since these funds are not in his tax-deferred IRA or 401(k) accounts, the tax bite may actually be controlling his decision.

2 Downshift for retirement. Clint's instincts are already telling him to begin downshifting. So far he's used what I call an "Aggressive Growth" model portfolio, with 90 percent in the stock categories. In the past he was building solely for the future without needing current income from his portfolio. It's obvious that Clint is beginning to anticipate the near future, when the regular paychecks stop and he must rely solely on his portfolio (plus any pensions and Social Security). That's his real motivation. In short, when he does retire, he'll need a portfolio that's less aggressive than it has been in the past decade and more focused on capital preservation and steady income.

Over the next decade, he may want to gradually shift more funds out of the aggressive-growth and into the growth area, while increasing his holdings in the fixed-income fund area, possibly even going to as much as 40 to 60 percent bonds. Doing so may cause more of a psychological than an economic shock, given his current aggressive portfolio.

Moreover, given today's longevity projections, Clint also knows that he must plan ahead if he wants to maintain his retirement in style for the next couple of decades or more. That could be four or five bull/bear cycles, filled with ups and downs, corrections and booms, and inflation. So, depending on his future income needs and his life-style, he may need to keep some of his portfolio in growth funds.

This investor has excellent fund-picking instincts. If he plans ahead and gradually rebalances his portfolio over the next few years, he can truly retire in style and with peace of mind.

EXAMPLE #5:
NEW MILLENNIUM RETIREES

Aggressive strategy designed to beat inflation. . . .

MOST INVESTMENT planners and almost all electronic planning tools will advise you to start switching out of stocks and into fixed-income funds before retirement. I now believe that this strategy might be too conservative and prove costly in some cases for the retiree who is unable to beat inflation. Why? "The life expectancy of the typical 55-year-old woman today is more than 82 years, meaning that a portion of your cash must last at least 27 years. By any measure, 27 years is long-term investing," says *Money* magazine.

Similarly, a CBS MarketWatch reader recently criticized me for suggesting a retirement portfolio with a large allocation to fixed-income funds: "The average number of years that the surviving spouse will live beyond age 65 is 25 years. Moreover, a *Mutual Funds* magazine article points out that folks must take risks even at 65 and 70. Otherwise your Income Preservation portfolio is going to become an 'Income Decliner'! No portfolio should be 100 percent in Income Preservation or Conservative Income. It's too risky."

Thanks to modern medical advances and longevity, today's retirees are being forced to play by a new set of rules: Today all retirees are long-term investors and also more aggressive investors. In fact, you have no choice but to branch out if you want to beat inflation.

Here's one inspiring example from Rocky, a "new millennium" retiree who sounds more like a cocky 25-year-old than someone who is approaching the 75-year marker:

> I am, after all, 75 years old. Yesterday, I passed my flight physical for the 15th year after heart surgery. I just hung up the skis last week after skiing twice a week for the past 6 months (my 65th season). I quit work about 3 years ago after my third entrepreneurial career, although I play at investing as hard as I used to work. I fly my own plane on most vacations, although we did drive to Alaska 2 years ago and spent last fall in Europe.

How does he live like that on a relatively frugal budget? He has a well-planned investment strategy:

> My investment strategy has been to use:
> [1] A high-quality junk bond fund to generate cash flow, using the growth to replace the withdrawals
> [2] Several aggressive growth funds of assorted capitalization sizes
> [3] About 10 percent conservative bonds
> [4] A small amount of international stocks
> [5] Money markets
> [6] About 3 percent of my money to day-trade on the high-tech market, which has only been modestly successful, mostly because I am not driven enough. Gotta get up with the birds for that game.
>
> I defend this ridiculously adventuresome posture on [the basis of] my willingness/desire to actively manage my money. If things go to hell, I can and will move decisively and quickly. And if I develop a more "elderly" frame of mind, more laissez-faire, then I guess I will have to move into a much more conservative posture.

Clearly, Rocky is not your average retired investor, as we saw earlier in Example #3. His strategy is not recommended for all seniors. The idea, however, is to review your financial plan, taking into account the number of years you think you'll need to live on the money in your portfolio. Your portfolio, even in retirement, shouldn't be 100 percent fixed-income because you'll need to keep pace with inflation.

Portfolio Alternatives: Out of the Box

HERE ARE SOME good ideas that will help you diversify your mutual fund portfolio, helping you learn and earn a little more along the way.

CHOOSING A TOTALLY indexed portfolio may seem un-conventional, but it's a low-cost, low-risk, low-stress option that actually performs better than about 80 to 90 percent of all funds. Indexing part or all of one's portfolio is becoming more and more popular. *Kiplinger's* recommends it. *Money* and *Mutual Funds* have touted its virtues.

TOTALLY INDEXED PORTFOLIOS

THERE ARE AROUND two hundred index funds, with over $250 billion in total assets. This is small change compared with the $5 trillion-plus locked up in all mutual funds. Yet index funds are a hot item, with about 150 new ones introduced in the past few years. Recently, investors were pouring 20 to 25 percent of their new investment money into the index funds.

Fortunately, these market clones do their job incredibly well. For example, the granddaddy and still front-runner, Vanguard's Index 500 Fund, has had an average annual return of about 16 percent for 15 years, beating 80 percent of the 260 diversified-equity stock funds with the same longevity.

Check out our list of the top-ten index funds. And if you're serious about adding some index funds to your portfolio, do a little comparison shopping. Find out what makes them tick. Research the specifics.

Here's how it can work for you: Simply take your asset allocations and plug in the top index funds that match the right peer-group categories. This may be the lowest-stress, lowest-risk solution to the problem of picking among 10,000-plus mutual funds in an era of information overload. If so many top financial periodicals are betting on a totally indexed portfolio, perhaps you should seriously consider this alternative.

SOCIALLY RESPONSIBLE INVESTING

UNTIL RECENTLY, socially responsible (or socially conscious) funds have been saddled with a bad image. But that's changing as these funds show investors that they do measure up. In reality, many socially responsible funds now generate very respectable returns—some even outperform the indexes.

Let's admit it: Values are important to most of us. Whether you're conservative or liberal, Republican or Democrat, you probably have some very strong convictions about a few things in life. For example, if you have a friend or relative who is or was afflicted with lung cancer, you probably believe that smoking is life-threatening. Therefore, you may not want your money invested in tobacco companies.

Or you may be actively opposed to companies with policies detrimental to women's rights, unfavorable to minorities, or harmful to animals. Perhaps you are strictly opposed to child labor, sweatshops, weapons manufacturing, the death penalty, violence in films, sexually explicit material on television, or any one of many other issues that run contrary to your moral, ethical, or religious convictions.

On the other hand, you may believe that your personal convictions should be separated from your investment strategies. The vast majority of investors can and do live with that kind of split personality.

DOING WELL
BY DOING GOOD

FORTUNATELY, THE TIDE is turning. Call it divine intervention, synchronicity, or just good karma: We're entering a new age of social consciousness, one that fits the theme of Paul Zane Pilzer's best-seller, *God Wants You to Be Rich*. Not only are more investors putting their money where their mouths are, many socially conscious funds are becoming top performers. The socially responsible funds even have their own trade association, Social Investment Forum, which recently released the following statement about improvements in its members' performance:

> In the strongest showing in recent memory for socially and environmentally responsible mutual funds, a solid 20 out of 32 mutual funds at least two years old tracked by the nonprofit Social Investment Forum earned the best possible rankings from either Lipper Analytical Services or Morningstar, or both. These outstanding results were earned by the funds in 1997, the same year that saw socially and environmentally responsible assets under professional management in the U.S. top the $1 trillion mark.
>
> According to the Social Investment Forum, 15 socially screened funds earned "A" or "B" rankings from Lipper based on total returns in their respective investment categories for the 12 months ended December 31, 1997. As of the end of 1997, a total of 12 screened funds carry four or five stars from Morningstar for risk-adjusted performance, which is based on a three-year analysis.

So the socially responsible *can* turn a profit. According to Social Investment Forum President Steve Schueth:

> It was a great year for social investing. . . . A lot of socially aware investors made a lot of money during 1997. The real-

world performance of socially screened funds and the academic evidence both conclusively show that concerned investors can have their cake and eat it too.

People can make money while helping to encourage more positive and healthy corporate behavior. With all this good news in hand, we expect even faster growth of responsibly invested fund assets in 1998.

According to a Social Investment Forum study released on November 5, 1997, assets in socially screened portfolios surged 227 percent from $162 billion to $529 billion over the past two years, sparked in large part by anti-tobacco sentiments. The Forum analysis concluded that the total volume of responsibly invested assets climbed from $639 billion to $1.185 trillion between 1995 and 1997, an increase of 85 percent.

Not bad when you realize that the total assets of all mutual funds are just over $5 trillion.

PUT YOUR MONEY
WHERE YOUR CONSCIENCE IS

ARE YOU READY TO invest with your conscience? The best place to start is the Social Investment Forum. This association actually posts a list of about fifty socially conscious funds. One you might check out to start is the Domini Social Equity Fund. This fund was rated five stars by Morningstar for the 3-year period ending December 1997, compared against 2,232 domestic equity funds.

In other words, many socially conscious funds are now competing favorably with the rest of the leading funds. There are no longer any excuses for separating your personal values and your investment strategies.

DRIPs: WALL STREET'S
BEST-KEPT SECRET!

IF YOU'RE FED UP WITH the fact that 80 to 90 percent of all mutual funds can't beat their indexes, if you want a more active role in picking stocks, and if you think you can do a better job than the pros, then start your own fund using DRIPs! That's the advice of Vita Nelson, editor of *MoneyPaper*, a newsletter dedicated to DRIPs, which she calls "the best-kept secret on Wall Street."

Dividend reinvestment programs—affectionately known as DRIPs—are investment opportunities offered directly to investors by many corporations. They enable shareholders to automatically reinvest cash dividends and capital gains distributions, thus accumulating more stock without paying any broker's fees. The best part is that many DRIPs also allow additional cash investments by the shareholder.

DRIPs are already offered by many major U.S. corporations. Today over a thousand major companies have DRIP programs. Most of them are the blue-chip members of the Dow Jones Industrial Average and S&P 500—companies like Coke, Exxon, General Electric, and Motorola, as well as some foreign companies, such as British Airways, Glaxo Wellcome, and SmithKline Beecham, through American depositary receipts.

CREATE YOUR OWN MUTUAL FUND AND SAVE

WITH DRIPS YOU CAN also save that 1.5 percent annual management fee you pay to a Wall Street full-service broker like Salomon Smith Barney. Moreover, you'll save another 1.4 percent in the operating expenses that the average fund manager charges. Best of all, you'll cut out your broker's commission. All that is "lost money" anyway.

How much more will be in your pocket? Lots! Think of it this way: Since 1926, stocks have returned an average of 10.5 percent. So if you save 3 to 4 percent on management and brokerage costs, the 10.5 percent is on the bottom line and in your bank account. That could mean a 30 percent or higher increase in your portfolio's return. Now that should motivate you to look at DRIPs more closely!

Joe Tigue, editor of Standard and Poor's *Dividend Reinvestment Plans Annual Directory,* says, "DRIPs have grown increasingly popular with individual investors. . . . [it's] a no-brainer. . . . many more will be seen before long as companies jump on the bandwagon. . . . a big attraction of DRIPs is the commission you save on brokers." In one of the tables in the S&P directory you'll see that if you had invested $1,000 in any one of the DRIP programs of seventy-five companies in 1985 (before the crash) your money would have been worth between $6,211 and $36,123 10 years later. Here's a sampling of ten of those stocks and the 10-year growth of an initial investment of $1,000:

- ◆ Franklin Resources $36,123
- ◆ Home Depot $26,855
- ◆ Computer Associates $20,582
- ◆ Fannie Mae $16,668
- ◆ Gillette $12,928
- ◆ Coca-Cola $12,203
- ◆ Caterpillar $8,959
- ◆ Johnson & Johnson $7,395
- ◆ Pep Boys $6,764
- ◆ Campbell's Soup $6,268

Did your fund do this well in the last decade? With all these advantages, DRIPs have to be the do-it-yourself investor's dream. No wonder the editor of *MoneyPaper* calls them the best-kept secret on Wall Street. And no wonder the SEC won't let corporations advertise them. If this secret gets out, brokers might go broke.

DRIPs OFFER AUTO-PILOT SAVINGS DISCIPLINE

IT'S SO EASY TO GET started investing in DRIPs. All you need is a single share of stock to start, and there are several organizations that sell single shares (see the Web sites listed in the Resources section of this book). Then you just enroll in the company's program and start sending them your monthly savings checks. You can even make it a painless automatic deduction from your bank account. This certainly is a no-brainer.

If the DRIP experts are right, building a diversified portfolio with DRIPs is a slam-dunk. Several great references on-line and in print will get you on track with a minimum of effort. The bible of the field, and a good place to start your reading, is Charles Carlson's how-to book, *No-Load Stocks*. Carlson, the king of DRIPs, also has a monthly newsletter, *DRIP Investor*. Here are five other leading sources of information on DRIPs:

◆ American Association of Individual Investors
◆ *DRIP Investor* newsletter
◆ *MoneyPaper* newsletter
◆ National Association of Investors Corporations
◆ Standard & Poor's *Dividend Reinvestment Plans Annual Directory*

DRIPs may, in fact, be the best investments you'll ever make in the stock market, although they lack the diversification mutual funds give you. Contact your favorite discount broker and ask them to help you get going.

Rebalancing Rules: How to Monitor Your Portfolio

MONITOR YOUR INVESTMENTS periodically. It's vital to revisit your portfolio annually to check on the status of your allocations and make sure your funds are performing as expected.

REBALANCING RULES

HERE ARE SEVERAL crucial rebalancing rules, according to the American Association of Individual Investors *Journal:*

◆ **Annual Rebalancing:** "Remember that rebalancing does not need to be frequent—annually is sufficient. However, your actual portfolio allocations will be constantly changing due to varying performances and as you withdraw funds."

◆ **Don't Stray Too Much:** "Don't worry about straying from your desired allocation by a few percentage points, but straying by 5 percent should start to become a concern, and straying 10 percent will have a major impact on your portfolio's return. In between that range—it's a tough decision and will likely be dictated by your personal tax situation and personal preferences."

◆ **Minimum Commitments:** "At least 10 percent of a portfolio must be committed to a market segment to have a meaningful impact" on your portfolio. "If your desired allocation to a particular asset class is only 10 percent, you would not want to stray below that amount by very much; in contrast, falling a few percentage points below a 30 percent desired level would be less of a concern."

IN THE EARLY 1980s THE American Association of Individual Investors (AAII) opened its doors and quickly became the Main Street investor's strongest supporter in an environment dominated by the big Wall Street institutional investors. Not long ago the AAII's *Journal* published an interesting article entitled "Portfolio Rebalancing and the 'Problem' with the Bull Market," which captured the essence of the rebalancing dilemma.

Here's the rebalancing "problem" in a nutshell. Let's assume you're an investor with a portfolio that includes $100,000 in stock funds (50 percent of the portfolio) and $100,000 in bond funds (the other 50 percent). For simplicity's sake, let's say the stocks have doubled in value

◆ **Discipline:** The AAII *Journal* emphasizes that "rebalancing provides a discipline: it forces you to sell high and buy low." In other words, when making specific rebalancing decisions, a savvy investor will take profits in the sales, while seeking value in the replacements.

◆ **Uncle Sam:** "If you do rebalance using taxable accounts, do so in a way to minimize taxes," looking closely at the basis of each share.

◆ **Don't Get Greedy:** If you have a portfolio of funds that have been very successful, "consider selective pruning of individual holdings that have done well." In short, stay focused on your overall portfolio, without falling in love with any particularly hot funds.

◆ **Focus on the Long Term:** "Enjoy the bull market while it lasts, but don't let several terrific years deflect you from a long-term strategy." In short, remember: The market does advance, but in cycles that go down as well as up. Plan your asset allocations for the long term through both phases.

to $200,000. This is a reasonable assumption, because the market is about double what it was a few years ago. Note, however, that your portfolio's asset allocations are now 67 percent in stocks and 33 percent in bonds, a 17 percent deviation from your original portfolio.

Depending upon your stage in life and your financial plan, this happy development may mean it is time to rebalance.

WHEN IS IT TIME TO DUMP A FUND?

LONG-TERM INVESTORS should only rebalance when truly necessary, for example

◆ When significant gains (such as those from the bull market) or major losses have skewed your intended allocations;

◆ When your investment objectives change;

◆ When you need to shift your portfolio into more fixed-income vehicles (bonds) as you enter retirement or plan to invest part of your savings for a shorter-term need;

◆ When a fund seems to be consistently and continually slipping compared with the benchmarks; or

◆ When a proven manager leaves a fund and you are unsure about the replacement.

Research shows us that rebalancing often accomplishes very little, except in extreme cases. In other words, take the time to choose your allocations correctly and stick with them unless you have a tangible reason to sell or reposition, such as taxes or college tuition for your teenagers. Charles Schwab & Company recently reported an interesting study that incorporated Morningstar research data. The study tested the various possibilities of when and what to sell off. Its conclusions favor this rule: Rebalance annually and sell only the bottom quartile of your holdings based on performance.

COMPARE TODAY'S ASSET ALLOCATIONS
WITH YOUR IDEAL PORTFOLIO

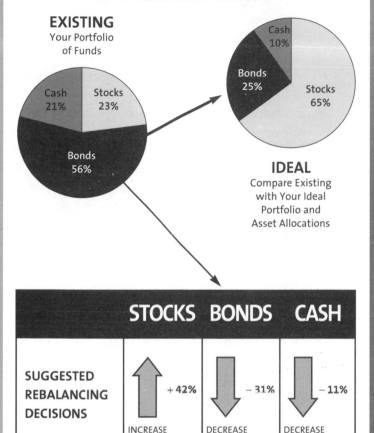

EXISTING
Your Portfolio
of Funds

Cash
21%

Stocks
23%

Bonds
56%

Cash
10%

Bonds
25%

Stocks
65%

IDEAL
Compare Existing
with Your Ideal
Portfolio and
Asset Allocations

	STOCKS	BONDS	CASH
SUGGESTED REBALANCING DECISIONS	⬆ + 42% INCREASE	⬇ − 31% DECREASE	⬇ − 11% DECREASE
TOTAL $100,000	+ $42,000	− $31,000	− $11,000

A simple lesson in rebalancing: let's say you now have 56 percent in bonds, 23 percent in stocks, and 21 percent in cash. But you determine that your ideal asset allocations are more aggressive: stocks 65 percent, bonds only 25 percent, and cash 10 percent. So you need to sell 31 percent of your existing bonds, reduce your cash by 11 percent, and increase your stock funds by 42 percent.

Monitoring your investments is an important part of portfolio maintenance, but remember that buy-and-hold investors are long-term strategists. Life has a strange and unpredictable habit of forcing us to rebalance our lives as well as our portfolios unexpectedly. Rebalancing is as natural as replacing an automobile or anything else that wears out or just falls apart.

Always remember as you reexamine and rebalance your investments to focus on your overall portfolio, not on the individual funds. Make it easy for yourself: Choose the funds from this book, or look on the CBS Market-Watch Web site (cbs.marketwatch.com) for an up-to-date list of these funds, then plug them into the asset allocation that makes the most sense for you and your family. Make adjustments when needed, and continue to educate yourself. And trust yourself. You can do it. Become a do-it-yourself investor.

Market cycles and our changing economic status are constantly altering our portfolios. Rebalance your portfolio so that it matches the asset allocations that are right for your lifestyle, and you will be able to do everything you want to in this lifetime, with money to spare and well-earned peace of mind.

EPILOGUE

DO-IT-YOURSELF INVESTING
BOLDLY GOES BEYOND
TECHNOLOGY

HOW WILL YOU be investing in the millennium?
Nobody really knows. But if I had to write the script,
the opening line would read something like this:
"Robots will be managing your portfolio very soon."
Yes, robots.

Actually, they'll be extensions of your portfolio, pro-
grammed by you, magnifying your analytical powers
by quantum leaps. They'll make it possible for everyone on Main Street America to be do-it-yourself
investors, to take total control of their financial destinies. These robots will replace many of the Wall
Street professionals on whom we used to rely to make
our financial decisions. Before long, the physical stock
exchanges will also disappear. A single global satellite

network, a one-to-one virtual exchange, will link all investors. Stay with me.

You turn on the television to watch one of your favorite programs. A familiar voice speaks in a calm tone: "Good evening, Paul. I see you're relaxed and enjoying the evening news. We have an update on your portfolio, along with a summary of today's markets. Would you like to go over it now or shall we wait until later?"

You check your watch: "Better do it now." The screen lights up: an attractive anchorperson then launches into a short summary of the day: market highlights, followed by a couple of alerts, an earnings report on a stock held by one of your funds, and news of a major change in management. After that, your entire portfolio—all of your security holdings—appears on the screen. You ask for more details.

The voice continues: "Paul, if you ask my advice, based on the most likely impact of these changes on your port-folio, I would recommend that you. . . ." And so it goes—your "robot" giving you advice on specific securities and recommendations on rebalancing your portfolio. Then it adds, "That stock has dropped below your 5 percent limit. There are some interested buyers in the Hong Kong mar-kets. Do you want to trade it now?"

Artificial intelligence? Talking computers running your portfolio for you? Am I carrying the principle of do-it-yourself investing too far, too fast? You think I'm making this up?

I'm not. Forget 2200 and the Starship *Enterprise*. It may happen as early as 2002, but certainly within the next decade. In fact, by 2010 everyone will be an on-line investor: everyone will be investing this way, thanks to the accelerating pace of cyberspace technologies. Absurd? No. Think back to just a few years ago.

I remember that as recently as 1995 most people would stare blankly when I mentioned stuff like the Net and http://. At that time there were fewer than 100,000 on-line investors. Today there are over five million out there, and the pace is accelerating. The stock market is becoming a virtual reality in cyberspace, not something physically located in New York City.

Innovations just keep moving us ahead. They will make it possible for the next generation of do-it-yourself investors to take total responsibility for their financial destinies, with user-friendly tools as much a part of our world as the fax, the photocopy, and the cell phone.

I was discussing this bold new future with an executive at E*Trade, one of those on-line discount brokers that, like Schwab and AmeriTrade, are now successfully competing with old-line Wall Street brokers like Merrill Lynch and Salomon Smith Barney. Remember E*Trade's ad slogan? "Someday we'll all invest this way." They made this bold prediction when fewer than 10 percent of all investors were on-line.

"New technologies are replacing old ones so fast," I said to him, "by 2010 not only will everyone be investing on-line, robots will be running their portfolios."

"By 2010?" he quickly replied. "We'll have one up by 2000!" That's how fast technology is accelerating this new paradigm. It looks as if the paradigm shift is not just a decade ahead of schedule: it's two centuries ahead.

Yes, someday we'll all invest this way. But that doesn't mean that we'll all be slaves to the PC. On-line investing is only the surface issue. A much bigger and more significant revolution is actually in progress. John Naisbitt put it succinctly in *The Global Paradox:* "The telecommunications revolution will enlarge the role of the individual with more access to information, greater speed of execution, and greater ability to communicate to anyone or to great numbers anywhere, anytime. All trends are in the direction of making the smallest player in the global economy more and more powerful."

New on-line technologies are empowering investors throughout the world, setting everyone free, including investors without computers. The playing field has leveled and investors are no longer dependent on Wall Street. Yes, someday we'll all be do-it-yourself investors controlling our own financial destinies.

Someday has arrived. Where's your robot?

RESOURCES

ULTIMATE WEB YELLOW PAGES
FOR MUTUAL FUNDS

INTERNET SITES WITH FREE MUTUAL FUND INFORMATION SOURCES

Financial Periodicals Reporting on Funds

Barron's	www.barrons.com
Bloomberg Personal Finance	www.bloomberg.com
BusinessWeek	www.businessweek.com
Forbes	www.forbes.com
Fortune	www.fortune.com
Individual Investor	www.individualinvestor.com
Kiplinger's	www.kiplinger.com
Money	www.money.com
Mutual Funds	www.mfmag.com
SmartMoney	www.smartmoney.com
USA Today	www.usatoday.com
U.S. News & World Report	www.usnews.com
The Wall Street Journal	www.wsj.com
Worth	www.worth.com

Financial News TV-Web Broadcasters

CBS.MarketWatch	cbs.marketwatch.com
CNBC	www.cnbc.com
CNNfn	www.cnnfn.com

Web Sites with Fund News and Data

Data Broadcasting Corporation	www.dbc.com
FundsInteractive	www.fundsinteractive.com
IBC Financial Data	www.ibcdata.com
Investment Company Institute	www.ici.org
Investorama	www.investorama.com/funds.html
PCQuote	www.pcquote.com

Quicken   www.quicken.com
Quotecom   www.quote.com
Yahoo   quote.yahoo.com

Mutual Fund Rating Agencies
CDA/Wiesenberger   www.cda.com
Institute for Econo-   www.mfmag.com
    metric Research
Lipper Inc.   www.lipperweb.com
Morningstar   www.morningstar.net
S&P/Micropal   www.micropal.com

Largest Mutual Fund Families
AIM   www.aimfunds.com
American Century   www.americancentury.
                                     com
American Express/IDS   www.americanexpress.com
American Funds   www.americanfunds.com
Dreyfus   www.dreyfus.com
Fidelity   www.fidelity.com
Franklin/Templeton   www.franklin-templeton.
                                     com
Janus   www.janusfunds.com
Kemper   www.kemper.com
Merrill Lynch   www.ml.com
MFS   www.mfs.com
Morgan Stanley   www.msdw.com
    Dean Witter
Oppenheimer   www.oppenheimerfunds.com
Prudential   www.prudential.com
Putnam   www.putnaminv.com
Salomon Smith Barney   www.salomonsmithbarney.
                                     com
Scudder   www.funds.scudder.com
T. Rowe Price   www.troweprice.com
Vanguard   www.vanguard.com
Van Kampen   www.van-kampen.com

Mutual Fund Supermarkets and Discount Brokers

AmeriTrade	www.accutrade.com
Discover Brokerage	www.dbdirect.com
DLJ Direct	www.dljdirect.com
E*Trade Mutual Funds Network	www.etrade.com
Fidelity FundsNetwork	www.fidelity.com
Jack White/Waterhouse	www.jackwhiteco.com
National Discount Brokers	www.ndb.com
Charles Schwab Mutual Fund OneSource	www.schwab.com
Muriel Siebert & Co.	www.msiebert.com

Corporate Profiles and Earnings

First Call	www.firstcall.com
Hoover's	www.hoovers.com
Zacks	www.zacks.com

Mutual Funds Education and Support

American Association of Individual Investors	www.aaii.org
Mutual Fund Education Alliance	www.mfea.com
National Association of Investors Corporation	www.better-investing.org
U.S. Securities & Exchange Commission	www.sec.gov

Web Search Engines

AltaVista	www.altavista.com
Excite	www.excite.com
Hotbot	www.hotbot.com
InfoSeek	www.infoseek.com
Lycos	www.lycos.com
Netscape	www.netscape.com
WebCrawler	www.webcrawler.com
Yahoo	www.yahoo.com

READING LIST

MUTUAL FUNDS INVESTING

BusinessWeek Guide to Mutual Funds, by Jeffrey Laderman (McGraw-Hill, 1998)

Buying Stocks Without a Broker, by Charles B. Carlson (McGraw-Hill, 1996)

Charles Schwab's Guide to Financial Independence, by Charles Schwab (Bantam Doubleday Dell, 1998)

The Complete Idiot's Guide to Making Money with Mutual Funds, by Alan Lavine and Gail Liberman (Alpha Books, 1998)

Die Broke, by Stephen Pollan (HarperCollins, 1997)

Ernst & Young's Total Financial Planner, by Robert Garner et al. (John Wiley & Sons, 1996)

Get a Financial Life, by Beth Kobliner (Fireside, 1996)

Handbook for No-Load Fund Investors, by Sheldon Jacobs (No-Load Fund Investors, 1998)

How to Make Money in Stocks, by William O'Neil (McGraw-Hill, 1994)

How to Retire Rich, by James O'Shaughnessy (Broadway Books, 1998)

Investing with Your Values, by Hal Brill, Jack A. Brill, and Cliff Feigenbaum (Bloomberg Press, 1999)

Market Wizards, by Jack Schwager (HarperBusiness, 1993)

The Money Club, by Marilyn Crockett and Diane Felenstein (Fireside, 1997)

The Money Drunk, by Mark Brian and Julia Cameron (Lowell House, 1992)

The Motley Fool Investment Guide, by Dave and Tom Gardner (Simon & Schuster, 1998)

Mutual Fund Buyer's Guide, by Norman Fosback (McGraw-Hill, 1998)

Mutual Funds for Dummies, by Eric Tyson (IDG Books, 1998)

Mutual Funds on the Net, by Paul B. Farrell (Wiley, 1997)

The New Commonsense Guide to Mutual Funds, by Mary Rowland (Bloomberg Press, 1998)

The New Market Wizards, by Jack Schwager (HarperBusiness, 1994)

The Nine Steps to Financial Freedom, by Suze Orman (Random House, 1997)

No-Load Stocks, by Charles Carlson (McGraw-Hill, 1995)

One Up on Wall Street, by Peter Lynch (Penguin, 1989)

The Only Investment Guide You'll Ever Need, by Andrew Tobias (Harcourt Brace, 1996)

A Random Walk Down Wall Street, by Burton Malkeil (W. W. Norton, 1995)

Ten Steps to Financial Prosperity, by Bill Griffeth (Probius, 1994)

The Wall Street Journal Guide to Understanding Money and Investing, by Kenneth Morris and Alan Siegel (Lightbulb Press/Simon & Schuster, 1993)

Your Money or Your Life, by Joe Dominguez and Vicki Robin (Viking, 1993)

WISE INVESTING AND SUCCESSFUL LIVING

The Artist's Way, by Julia Cameron (J. P. Tarcher, 1992). Within every investor is an artist. Discover yours, and find a new way to live successfully.

The Dilbert Future, by Scott Adams (HarperBusiness, 1998). Just in case you're taking life too seriously and it hurts, laughter is the best medicine.

Don't Worry, Make Money, by Richard Carlson (Hyperion, 1997). One hundred practical ways to achieve financial success by letting go of negative emotions, worry, anger, resentment, and fear.

Do What You Love, the Money Will Follow, by Marsha Sinetar (Dell, 1989). This book inspired me to change career paths.

Global Paradox, by John Naisbitt (Avon, 1995). My favorite vision of a future that is already here: "The telecommunications revolution. . . . all trends are in the direction of making the smallest player in the global economy more and more powerful." Also read Naisbitt's *Mega-*

trends series, with his comprehensive images of the next millennium, of Asia, and of women, and the original, *Megatrends.*

God Wants You to Be Rich, by Paul Zane Pilzer (Simon & Schuster, 1995). A practical solution for the skeptic who believes "It is much harder for a rich man to enter the Kingdom of God than for a camel to go through the eye of a needle."

The Inner Game of Trading, by Howard Abell and Robert Koppel (Probius, 1994). Experts only recently began discovering that making money depends 80 percent on your state of mind and only 20 percent on your methods, tools, data, and technologies. Here's one of the best explanations of this new approach.

The Instant Millionaire, by Mark Fisher (New World Library, 1991). An inspiring story of several meetings between a millionaire and an aspiring millionaire.

Seven Habits of Highly Effective People, by Stephen Covey (Simon & Schuster, 1989). A rational guide to achieving your goals while also helping the world around you.

The Seven Spiritual Laws of Success, by Deepak Chopra (Amber-Allen, 1995). Esoteric, yet very thought-provoking for anyone searching for more in life.

The Road Less Traveled, by M. Scott Peck (Touchstone, 1978). His opening lines on discipline have been the first step for many journeys: "Life is difficult. This is a great truth [one of the Buddha's Four Noble Truths]. It is a great truth because once we see the truth, we transcend it. Once we truly know that life is difficult—once we truly understand and accept it—then life is no longer difficult. Because once it is accepted, the fact that life is difficult no longer matters." Then life becomes an adventure!

Think and Grow Rich, by Napoleon Hill (Napoleon Hill Foundation, 1989). The classic on the "Science of Success" developed from the life and work of billionaire philanthropist Andrew Carnegie.

INDEX

[NOTE: Page numbers for entries occurring in figures are suffixed with an *f.*]

ABOUT BLOOMBERG

Bloomberg L.P., founded in 1981, is a global information services, news, and media company. Headquartered in New York, the company has nine sales offices, two data centers, and 80 news bureaus worldwide.

Bloomberg Financial Markets, serving customers in 100 countries around the world, holds a unique position within the financial services industry by providing an unparalleled combination of news, information, and analytic tools in a single package known as the BLOOMBERG® service. Corporations, banks, money management firms, financial exchanges, insurance companies, and many other entities and organizations rely on Bloomberg as their primary source of information.

BLOOMBERG NEWS℠, founded in 1990, offers worldwide coverage of economies, companies, industries, governments, financial markets, politics, and sports. The news service is the main content provider for Bloomberg's broadcast media, which include BLOOMBERG TELEVISION®— the 24-hour cable television network available in ten languages worldwide—and BLOOMBERG NEWS RADIO™—an international radio network anchored by flagship station BLOOMBERG NEWS RADIO AM 1130℠ in New York.

In addition to the BLOOMBERG PRESS® line of books, Bloomberg publishes *BLOOMBERG® MAGAZINE*, *BLOOMBERG PERSONAL FINANCE™*, and *BLOOMBERG WEALTH MANAGER™*.

To learn more about Bloomberg, call a sales representative at:

Frankfurt:	49-69-920-410	San Francisco:	1-415-912-2960
Hong Kong:	852-977-6000	São Paulo:	5511-3048-4500
London:	44-171-330-7500	Singapore:	65-438-8585
New York:	1-212-318-2000	Sydney:	61-29-777-8686
Princeton:	1-609-279-3000	Tokyo:	81-3-3201-8900

ABOUT THE AUTHOR

Paul B. Farrell, J.D., Ph.D., is the mutual funds editor of CBS MarketWatch, where he writes the "Farrell-on-Funds" column and maintains the SuperStar Funds database. He is the author of three previous books on investing and has been an investment banker with Morgan Stanley, associate editor at *The Los Angeles Herald-Examiner,* and chief operating officer of the Financial News Network.